The Gothic Literature and History of New England

ANTHEM STUDIES IN GOTHIC LITERATURE

Anthem Studies in Gothic Literature incorporates a broad range of titles that undertake rigorous, multi-disciplinary and original scholarship in the domain of Gothic Studies and respond, where possible, to existing classroom/ module needs. The series aims to foster innovative international scholarship that interrogates established ideas in this rapidly growing field, to broaden critical and theoretical discussion among scholars and students, and to enhance the nature and availability of existing scholarly resources.

Series Editor
Carol Margaret Davison – University of Windsor, Canada

The Gothic Literature and History of New England

Secrets of the Restless Dead

Faye Ringel

ANTHEM PRESS

Anthem Press
An imprint of Wimbledon Publishing Company
www.anthempress.com

This edition first published in UK and USA 2022
by ANTHEM PRESS
75–76 Blackfriars Road, London SE1 8HA, UK
or PO Box 9779, London SW19 7ZG, UK
and
244 Madison Ave #116, New York, NY 10016, USA

British Library Cataloguing-in-Publication Data
A catalogue record for this book is available from the British Library.

Library of Congress Control Number: 2021952771

ISBN-13: 978-1-78527-903-4 (Pbk)
ISBN-10: 1-78527-903-3 (Pbk)

Cover Image: Image of Pompe Stevens' Gravestone. Photograph by Louis Walker III,
provided by Charles Roberts, Director, Rhode Island Slave History Medallion project.

This title is also available as an e-book.

The Rhode Island Slave History Medallion organization is a public awareness program
committed to marking those historic sites connected to the history of slavery in Rhode
Island. The medallion for this ongoing project to commemorate Rhode Island's Slave
History incorporates the "winged soul" design of Pompe Stevens, who carved the stone
shown on the cover, located in the Common Burying Ground, Farewell Street, Newport,
Rhode Island. The text on the stone reads: "This stone was cut by Pompe Stevens in
Memory of His Brother Cuffe Gibbs who died in 1768." It is one of few gravestones
signed by an enslaved African American carver.

To the Monsters who scare us; who *are* us

CONTENTS

ACKNOWLEDGMENTS

Land Acknowledgment: This book was composed on land stolen from the Royal Mohegan Burial Ground, reserved by Uncas, Sachem of the Mohegans, in perpetuity from the "Nine-Mile Square" he provided to the English colonists in 1659.

Thank you to Lucy Maziar and the US Coast Guard Academy Library for extending off-campus access privileges to Professors Emeriti.

Thank you to my editors, Anna Maria Trusky and Carol Margaret Davison.

CHRONOLOGY

	Literary Event	Historical Event
1617–19		Epidemics devastate indigenous people of coastal New England
1619		First Africans enslaved in North America land in Virginia
1620		Pilgrims arrive in New England
1637	Thomas Morton, *The New English Canaan*	Pequot massacre and enslavement
1662	Michael Wigglesworth, *Day of Doom*	
1663	John Eliot, *Wampanoag Bible*	Cotton Mather b.
1675–76		King Philip's War
1684	Increase Mather, *Remarkable Providences*	
1692		Salem Witch Trials begin
1693	C. Mather, *Wonders of the Invisible World*	Salem Witch Trials end
1699	C. Mather, *Decennium Luctuosum*	
1702	C. Mather, *Magnalia Christi Americana*	
1703		Jonathan Edwards b.
1728		Cotton Mather d.
1741	Edwards, "Sinners in the Hands of an Angry God"	
1758		Jonathan Edwards d.
1771		Charles Brockden Brown b.
1776		US Declaration of Independence
1783		Treaty of Paris ends the Revolutionary War
1787	Philip Freneau, "The Indian Burying-Ground"	US Constitution signed
1791		Lydia Huntley Sigourney b.

	Literary Event	Historical Event
1793		John Neal b.
1799	Brown, *Edgar Huntly*	
1802		Lydia Maria Child b.
1803		Sarah Helen Whitman b.
1804		Nathaniel Hawthorne b.
1807		John Greenleaf Whittier b.
		Henry Wadsworth Longfellow b.
1809		Edgar Allan Poe b.
1811		Harriet Beecher Stowe b.
1812–15		US war with Britain
1813		Epes Sargent b.
1817	Neal, *Keep Cool*	
1819		Herman Melville b.
1822	Catherine M. Sedgwick, *A New-England Tale*	
1824	Child, *Hobomok*	
1827		Rose Terry Cooke b.
1828	Neal, *Rachel Dyer*	
1830		Emily Dickinson b.
1832	Hawthorne, "Roger Malvin's Burial"	
1834	Sigourney, "The Mohegan Church"	
1835	Hawthorne, "Young Goodman Brown"	Harriet Prescott Spofford b.
		Louisa May Alcott b.
1837		William Dean Howells b.
1838	Poe, *The Narrative of Arthur Gordon Pym of Nantucket*	
		Annie Trumbull Slosson b.
1841	Ralph Waldo Emerson, "Self-Reliance"	
1843	Longfellow, "Skeleton in Armor"	Henry James b.
	George Perkins Marsh, "The Goths in New England"	
1847	Whittier, *Supernaturalism of New England*	
	D. P. Thompson, *Locke Amsden*	Madeline Yale Wynne b.
1849		Sarah Orne Jewett b.

	Literary Event	Historical Event
1850	Hawthorne, *The Scarlet Letter*	
1851	Melville, *Moby-Dick*	
	Hawthorne, *The House of the Seven Gables*	
1852	Stowe, *Uncle Tom's Cabin*	Mary E. Wilkins Freeman b.
1856	Melville, *Benito Cereno*	
1857		Alice Brown b.
1858	Rose Terry Cooke, "My Visitation"	
1860	Spofford, "Circumstance"	Charlotte Perkins Gilman b.
	Whitman, *Edgar Poe and His Critics*	
1861–65		American Civil War
1861		Louise Imogen Guiney b.
1862		Edith Wharton b.
1864	Sargent, *Peculiar*	Nathaniel Hawthorne d.
1865	Whittier, *Snowbound*	Abraham Lincoln assassinated
		Lydia Huntley Sigourney d.
1868	Elizabeth Stuart Phelps Ward, *The Gates Ajar*	
1872	Stowe, *Sam Lawson's Oldtown Fireside Stories*	
1873	Phelps Ward, "Since I Died"	
1874		Robert Frost b.
		Amy Lowell b.
1876		John Neal d.
1878		Sarah Helen Whitman d.
1880	Howells, *The Undiscovered Country*	Lydia Maria Child d.
		Epes Sargent d.
1886	James, *The Bostonians*	Emily Dickinson d.
1888		Louisa May Alcott d.
1890		H. P. Lovecraft b.
1891		Herman Melville d.
1892	Gilman, "The Yellow Wall-paper"	John Greenleaf Whittier d.
		Henry Wadsworth Longfellow d.
		Rose Terry Cooke d.

	Literary Event	Historical Event
1895	Wynne, "The Little Room"	
1896	Jewett, *Country of the Pointed Firs*	Harriet Beecher Stowe d.
1897	A. Brown, "There and Here"	
1898	Slosson, *Dumb Foxglove and Other Stories*	
1902	Wilkins Freeman, "Luella Miller"	
1906	Guiney, *A Roadside Harp*	
1909		Sarah Orne Jewett d.
1911	Wharton, *Ethan Frome*	
1913	Josephine Dodge Daskam Bacon, "The Gospel"	
1914	Frost, *North of Boston*	World War I begins
1915	Frost, *A Boy's Will*	
1916		Shirley Jackson b.
		Henry James d.
1917		United States enters World War I
		Robert Lowell b.
1918		Armistice; Spanish flu pandemic
		Madeline Yale Wynne d.
1920		Louise Imogen Guiney d.
		William Dean Howells d.
1921		Harriet Prescott Spofford d.
1923	Amy Lowell, "A Dracula of the Hills"	
1924		Immigration Act imposes quotas
1925		Amy Lowell d.
1926		Annie Trumbull Slosson d.
		James Merrill b.
1927	Lovecraft, *The Case of Charles Dexter Ward* (published posthumously)	
1928	Esther Forbes, *A Mirror for Witches*	
1929		Stock market crash, Great Depression begins
1930		Mary E. Wilkins Freeman d.
1931		Toni Morrison b.

	Literary Event	Historical Event
1935		Charlotte Perkins Gilman d.
1936	Lovecraft, "Shadow over Innsmouth"	
	Stephen Vincent Benét, "The Devil and Daniel Webster"	
1937		H. P. Lovecraft d.
		Edith Wharton d.
1939–45		World War II
1941		United States enters World War II
1946	Robert Lowell, *Lord Weary's Castle*	
1947		Stephen King b.
1948	Jackson, "The Lottery"	Alice Brown d.
1953	Arthur Miller, *The Crucible*	
1959	Jackson, *The Haunting of Hill House*	
1962	Jackson, *We Have Always Lived in the Castle*	
1963		Robert Frost d.
1965		Shirley Jackson d.
1975	Alcott, *Behind a Mask: The Unknown Thrillers*	
1977		Robert Lowell d.
1982	Charles L. Grant, *The Soft Whisper of the Dead*	
	Merrill, *The Changing Light at Sandover*	
1983	King, *Pet Sematary*	
1986	King, *It*	
1990	Joseph A. Citro, *The Unseen*	
	Morrison, *Beloved*	
1992	Morrison, *Playing in the Dark*	
1994	King, "The Man in the Black Suit"	
1995		James Merrill d.
1998	King, *Bag of Bones*	
2001		9/11 Attacks; "War on Terror" begins
2004	Marilyn Nelson, *Fortune's Bones: The Manumission Requiem*	

	Literary Event	Historical Event
2008		Great financial crisis begins
2009	Caitlin R. Kiernan, *The Red Tree*	
	Joe Hill, Gabriel Rodriguez, *Locke & Key. Vol. 1 Welcome to Lovecraft*	
2012	Rick Hautala, *Untcigahunk—the Complete Little Brothers*	
	Andrea Hairston, *Redwood and Wildfire*	
2013	Susan Stinson, *Spider in a Tree*	
	Liz Duffy Adams, *Wonders of the Invisible World*	
2015	Robert Eggers, director, *The Witch: A New-England Folktale*	
2016	Matt Ruff, *Lovecraft Country*	Black Lives Matter protests begin
2017	Jordan Peele, director, *Get Out*	
	Ruthanna Emrys, *Winter Tide*	
2019		Toni Morrison d.
2020	Paul Tremblay, *Survivor Song*	COVID-19 pandemic begins; Black Lives Matter protests intensify
2021	W. S. Winslow, *The Northern Reach*	Invasion of the US Capitol

INTRODUCTION

The DEVIL, is more desirous to Regain poor *New England*, than any one
American spot of ground.
—Cotton Mather, *The Short History of New-England*
(1694); emphasis in original

Old graveyards are found throughout the New England landscape. Gravestones
like the one on the cover, its winged head symbolizing escape from the flesh,
remind us of the Puritans for whom this was the sole allowable form of figura-
tive art. In symbol and words, these gravestones are *memento mori*: remember,
as I am, so shall you be. Sometimes—as with Cuffe Gibbs's stone in Newport's
Common Burying Ground, signed by its carver Pompe Stevens—they express
pride in survival. Given the Puritans' contempt for the body, their rebellion
against the Catholic and Anglican concept of "hallowed ground" meant
that their family lands were often their last resting places. For the poor, the
enslaved, the displaced, there are few markers.

Though their passing may have left no trace, the dead are restless and the
world is changing. Hidden languages are emerging, rising again like rocks
after the winter. Wampanoag, Mohegan, and other Algonquian peoples are
reviving their once-lost languages, reminding us that the first Bible entirely
printed in North America was John Eliot's Wampanoag Bible. Rhode Island
is acknowledging its secrets of slavery with medallions like the "stumbling
stones" (*Stolpersteine*) Germany uses to mark houses where its slaughtered Jews
once lived.[1] In the Gothic mode, the past is ever present, and nothing buried
can remain undisturbed—not sins, bodies, or secrets.

For nearly fifty years, I have been addressing historical societies, family associations, and other genteel New England audiences, telling them the stories
they did not want to know about their ancestors and their contemporaries.
I'm rarely invited back. The descendants of New England's founders have

---

1. See *Rhode Island Slave History Medallions* for the Rhode Island project. Connecticut has a
similar project underway whose markers are modeled (with permission) on Germany's
stumbling stones. See *Witness Stones Project*. For more about Pompe Stevens's stone, see
Hopkins; Watters.

more than their share of family secrets. The Hale Family Reunion in Beverly, Massachusetts, in 1992 did not want to hear what Reverend Hale in 1692 said about women as witches. According to the docent at the John Brown House in Providence, home of the first benefactor of Brown University: "If you say your ancestor was in the Caribbean Trade, it was slaves; the China Trade, opium." (Brown's wealth came from both trades.) The Gothic mode is about abjection; in Julia Kristeva's terms, "what is abject, [...] the jettisoned object, is radically excluded" (2). Witches, slaves, the poor, and other objects of persecution and oppression may be cast out and excluded, but they can haunt us. The written and visual New England Gothic narratives studied here embody the repression, anxieties, and hypocrisy of four centuries of New England's history and the literature that emerged from it of hauntings, immurement, repression, and revenge.

Chapter 1, "Gothic Origins," explores the Gothic in literature and life, with an overview of the genre, its practitioners, and its critics in America and New England from its origins to the present, showing how America's equivalent of the genre's fantastic Middle Ages derives from the Puritans who transplanted Europe's nightmares to the New World, demonizing the indigenous peoples and projecting their fears upon European settlers of other religions, women, and Blacks.

Chapter 2, "The Puritans' Haunted Frontier," surveys Puritan texts and sermons of monsters, the devil, phantom invaders, and witch hunts. Frontier Gothic, usually linked to the American West, originated in Puritan fears of the wilderness and of attacks by the native peoples, reflected in accounts of King Philip's War and narratives of Indian captivity. The Puritans' apocalyptic mindset and their belief in witchcraft and demonic possession inspired American novelists from John Neal to the better-known Melville and Hawthorne in the American Renaissance to Stephen King and other horror writers of the late twentieth century.

Chapter 3, "Haunting the Master's House," focuses on the Domestic Gothic including supernatural and naturalistic fiction produced by feminists Harriet Beecher Stowe, Charlotte Perkins Gilman, and many other "local-color writers" as well as the rise of Spiritualism and the fiction inspired by that movement, with an excursus into the Gothic verse of canonical poets including Emily Dickinson. The tradition culminates in the twentieth century in New England Gothic's presiding genius, Shirley Jackson.

Chapter 4, "Beyond Lovecraft Country," reveals another skeleton in New England's Gothic closet—slavery and an enduring racism, manifested in the twentieth century in the eugenics movement and xenophobia. All can be found in the works of Providence writer Howard Phillips (H. P.) Lovecraft.

Today's writers of the Gothic and their readers are questioning and revising the racist and misogynistic narratives of Lovecraft and his disciples.

Through this Gothic lens, New England is a howling wilderness, besieged by the forces of Satan. Beginning with the Pilgrims who dug up the graves they found and removed the goods, the entire region can be seen effectively as a desecrated Indian burial ground. New England and indeed the United States can be figured as a haunted house, with madwomen screaming in the attic, the bones of Indians under the foundation, and African enslaved people in the basement, their skeletons in the closets. It is the old stone house on the hill. It is the abandoned farmhouse. It is dangerous entertainment.

Chapter 1

GOTHIC ORIGINS

There appeared unto him a Black-Man, of a Terrible aspect, and more than humane Dimensions, threatening bitterly to kill him.
—Calef, *Another Brand* (1697)

"Once in my life I met the Black Man! […] This scarlet letter is his mark!"
—Hester Prynne, Hawthorne, *The Scarlet Letter* (1850)

The earliest English settlers of New England feared a Black Man in the forests. Whether visualized as an Indian, an African, or a specter or Satan, this figure haunts the history and literature of the region. The Puritans brought the belief that the devil ruled the wilderness from the Old World into the forests of the new. Fear of this Black Man, symbolic or literal, can be found in Cotton Mather, whose witch cult's devil is Black; in Hawthorne's "Young Goodman Brown" (1835), which recounts one such forest meeting; and in Stephen King's homage to Hawthorne, "The Man in the Black Suit" (1994). In the last-mentioned story, the devil encounters the 9-year-old narrator who escapes and, unlike Young Goodman Brown, does not lose his faith or the woman he loves (his mother). But at the end of his long life, he fears that the pale white man in the Black Suit whose eyes burn in his head will return: "And in the dark I sometimes hear that voice drop even lower, into ranges which are inhuman. *Big fish!* It whispers in tones of hushed greed, and all the truths of the moral world fall to ruin before its hunger" (67; emphasis in original).

Before the term "Gothic romance" was coined, the original English settlers imposed an apocalyptic and horrific worldview on the new land. Puritan divines created "taproot texts": sermons, accounts of monstrous births and Satanic pacts, narratives of Indian captivity, and more that would inspire later writers of Gothic fiction, poetry, and drama.[1] Though for many years "American Gothic" meant Grant Wood's painting, or the Southern Gothic of Faulkner and Flannery O'Connor, today's critics agree that it began in New

---

1. I have applied this term coined by critic John Clute, "texts composed or written before those we can legitimately call fantasy," to narratives composed before the Gothic genre was named in the eighteenth century.

England. As Vermont folklorist and novelist Joseph A. Citro states, "The New England Gothicists can be credited with formulating an American sense of the supernatural. They brought New England wonders to the whole world" (*Passing* 11). How does the American Gothic stand out from the novels of Britain's first Gothic Revival? Allan Lloyd-Smith designates "four indigenous features" that distinguish the American Gothic tradition: "the frontier, the Puritan legacy, race and political utopianism" (2000: 109). To these I would add apocalypticism: all had their origins in New England. Jeffrey Weinstock sets out another four genres of the American Gothic found in America's pioneer Gothic novelist, Charles Brockden Brown: frontier, urban, psychological, and female (*Charles* 6). These genres, too, can be found in the New England Gothic tradition. The destruction of the indigenous peoples and the enslavement of African peoples haunted succeeding generations of writers who revealed secrets of the restless dead.

The Puritans transplanted Europe's nightmares to the New World, fearing the indigenous people as devil worshippers in the forest. Believing themselves to be the special targets of Satan for invading his kingdom, they reacted with paranoia directed against European settlers of other religions, women, and Blacks. New England's Puritan settlers envisioned themselves as the "new Israelites," with utopian visions of a City on a Hill. At the same time, ministers saw a fallen world and accused each new generation of backsliding from the theocratic state of their fathers. When a snake crawled into a Cambridge synod, Governor John Winthrop recorded it in his journal for 1648 as an omen: "The serpent is the devil" (2: 347). Haunting our narrative, Cotton Mather is author, folklorist, Fellow of the Royal Society, motivator of Gothic events, and character of Gothic romance. As Hawthorne describes him in "Alice Doane's Appeal," "a figure on horseback, so darkly conspicuous, so sternly triumphant" looking like "the visible presence of the fiend himself; but it was only his good friend Cotton Mather" (175).

The Puritans' fear of the untamed wilderness of their new home exemplifies what ecocritic Simon Estok calls "ecophobia": "an irrational and groundless hatred of the natural world [...] it is about power and control; it is what makes looting and plundering of animal and nonanimal resources possible" (208). So thoroughly did the Puritans and their descendants clear the wilderness that New England residents suffered their first energy crisis in the early 1800s, lacking wood for heating. Joe Hill's short-short story "Dead-Wood" (2007) haunts a Maine inn with the ghost of its state nickname, the pine tree: "no guest would stay the night there [...] their sleep was disturbed by the keening rush of a phantom wind, the low soft roar of air in high branches" (205).

The United States of America and the Gothic novel had their origins in the same movement: the Enlightenment. The philosophy and worldview that brought forth "a more perfect Union" also produced its opposite, the dark descent into fantasies of a past or present both thrilling and horrific. The Middle Ages, from which Enlightenment science and reason sought to rescue the world, became instead a source of horrific fascination in *The Castle of Otranto* (1764). Horace Walpole extended the Gothic in literature to life in his dream castle of Strawberry Hill. Gothic fiction exploded in the 1790s, with the international popularity of Lewis's *The Monk* and the "explained" Gothic of Mrs. Radcliffe. For American Gothic, the dead hand of the past is not represented by evil aristocrats exploiting the peasantry or by corrupt monks and the Inquisition, but by the secrets of a nation founded upon Enlightenment ideals that had persecuted and wiped out the native population and whose prosperity depended upon the enslavement and continued oppression of African Americans.

The new republic's citizens devoured the works of Britain's Gothic novelists, importing large quantities of novels and abridged "shilling shockers." Booksellers' figures support these contentions: Gothics were the most popular printed imports from the 1790s to 1820 (Ringe 14). Though barely a trace remains—they were read to shreds—testimony from clergy, politicians, and reviewers attests to the popularity of these "imported vices." In 1790, the Reverend Enos Hitchcock decries "the dangerous tendency of bad books" in *Memoirs of the Bloomsgrove Family*, an epistolary novel-polemic. Hitchcock prays, "May this *rising empire* cease to import" Gothic romances (2: 186–87, 193; emphasis in original). Devotees of the Gothic mode sought out romances set on this continent. One early best seller *The Asylum: Or, Alonso and Melissa. An American Tale, Founded on Fact* (1811) imported a castle along with dungeons, cruel aristocratic fathers, loyal *famuli* and simple peasants to the Connecticut colony. The anonymous author is usually identified as Isaac Mitchell, a journalist of Poughkeepsie, New York. In this novel, a father parts the titular lovers by immuring his daughter: "The mansion was of real Gothic architecture, built of rude stone with battlements" (2: 59). Within its walls, Melissa is tormented by frightening apparitions, later explained as the work of a gang of smugglers and thieves. A footnote warns readers against engaging in Gothic tourism because the castle had been destroyed in the Revolutionary War.

From the 1790s through the 1820s, intellectuals of the new republic struggled to define and create a separate identity for its literature, inspiring the theory that came to be called American Exceptionalism. Writers lamented the lack of suitable settings for Romance in this nation without a Middle Ages. The anonymous author of the first vampire fiction published in North America, *The Black Vampyre* (1819), a short novel "inspired by" Polidori's *The Vampyre*, concludes with this trope (though he had just written a supernatural Gothic romance set in America and Haiti): "In this happy land of liberty and equality, we are free from all traditional superstitions, whether political, religious, or otherwise. Fiction has no materials for machinery;—Romance no horrors for a tale of mystery" (D'Arcy 41). Whittier argued in his *Supernaturalism of New England* (1847) that the region, though devoid of a Gothic Middle Ages, with "no towers and castles over whose moonlight ruins gathers the green pall of the ivy," was yet hospitable to poetic fancy. "New-England is full of Romance [...] the great forest [...] the red men—their struggle and their disappearance—the Powwow and the War-dance [...] the tale of superstition, and the scenes of Witchcraft" (35).

Novelists agreed that the frontier and the treatment of the native peoples were the most appropriate subjects for American literature. In the preface to *Edgar Huntly; or, Memoirs of a Sleepwalker*, Charles Brockden Brown disdains "puerile superstition and exploded manners; Gothic castles and chimeras" and declares that "the incidents of Indian hostility, and the perils of the Western wilderness are far more suitable," for novels set in America (iii–iv). Although Brown, known as America's first Gothic novelist, came from the mid-Atlantic states, his contemporaries in New England followed his use of native landscape and frontier narratives; they also reflected conservative fears of conspiracy in the aftermath of the French Revolution. An explained Gothic romance, *Julia, and the Illuminated Baron* (1800) published by a "Lady from Massachusetts" (later identified as Sally S. B. K. Wood), placed an American heroine in the clutches of the French Illuminati.[2]

James Fenimore Cooper followed Brown's dictum: he drew on colonial Indian wars in *The Last of the Mohicans* (1826), which transplants legends of the Mohegan–Narragansett wars in the 1650s to New York's Mohawk Valley a century later, and in *The Wept of Wish-ton-Wish* (1829), a lengthy account of King Philip's War. Neither contains a hint of the supernatural, though they exemplify other aspects of the Frontier Gothic. John Neal, less known today, predates Cooper in combining Indians and the Gothic. Teresa Goddu in *Gothic America: Narrative, History, and Nation* (1997) argues that Neal should be considered "the voice of America's literary independence," "fill[ing] a gap in the genealogy of American Gothicism that begins with Brown and reaches its apogee with Poe" (72). Born and educated in Maine, Neal set most of his accounts of the Indian wars outside the region, though his weird tale "David Whicher" (published anonymously in 1832) is set in "Maine, always a frontier State" (353).

---

2. For an overview of American history in the light of conspiracy theory, see Goldberg.

At the center of the nineteenth century, Nathaniel Hawthorne and Herman Melville published two works central to the American literary canon: *The Scarlet Letter* (1850) and *Moby-Dick* (1851). Both works were composed in Massachusetts: New Yorker Melville then residing in Pittsfield and Hawthorne in Salem. The novels form an encyclopedia of Gothic themes: ecophobia, fear of the wilderness of land and sea; exile and conquering the unknown; women feared or erased; the sins of the fathers; and genocide of the native peoples. Melville's *Pequod* was named for "a celebrated tribe of Massachusetts Indians; now extinct as the ancient Medes" (76)—and apocalypticism—the white whale as Leviathan and the utopian Kingdom of God at sea formed by the *Pequod*'s multicultural crew. Gothic characters abound: Hawthorne's alchemist Chillingworth, the witch Mistress Hibbins, the persecuted yet stalwart heroine Hester, the unearthly child Pearl—sprite, demon, or angel in turn; Melville's obsessed hero-villain Captain Ahab, the wanderer called Ishmael, the Negro cabin boy Pip—the mad visionary who "saw God's foot on the treadle of the loom" (462). Hawthorne and Melville—together with Edgar Allan Poe—define a male tradition of the American Gothic.

In New England, from the 1820s onward, a women's tradition of Gothic regionalism flourished. Women published Frontier Gothic, sensational novels, and supernatural stories. The women's "local color" tradition of ghost stories flourished into the twentieth century, then was neglected until feminist scholars began to rediscover them in the 1970s.

The 1970s also saw the advent of Stephen King and a "horror boom" inspired by his success. Before this, Lovecraft had imposed his own fears of dissolution and devolution upon an imagined New England of abandoned farms and decaying seaports. It took King's stories and the films derived from them to make New England *the* locus of terror in the popular imaginary. For almost fifty years, Stephen King has portrayed a haunted New England, reflecting its history and folklore of Puritan paranoia, racism, class divides, abandonment of farming and industry, distrust of outsiders, and resistance to change. He is arguably America's best-known writer, shaping the way the world sees this country. As his chronicler Tony Magistrale notes in *Stephen King: America's Storyteller*, King expresses "the very real anxieties about how Americans live and where we are going, as a nation and as individuals. […] Stephen King has supplied America with a national portrait" (ix). At the same time, other New England residents writing regionalist horror have been ignored by critics. Writers from all over the world continue to set stories in Lovecraft's imagined New England. Most recently, women writers of the dark fantastic have begun responding to this mainly male tradition, deconstructing Lovecraft's mythos and rewriting folk horror set in New England.[3]

From television to film to social media, horror is at home in New England. Bernice Murphy's *The Rural Gothic in American Popular Culture: Backwoods Horror and Terror in the Wilderness* highlights the indie film *YellowBrickRoad* (2010), a wilderness Gothic similar to *The Blair Witch Project*, but set in New Hampshire, exemplifying folk horror and ecophobia. Jordan Peele's *Get Out* (2017) locates its racist horror not in the wilderness or in the South but in an affluent Connecticut suburb.

From this swift overview, we can discern certain continuing conflicts. Fear of the native peoples and guilt over their fate can be found in Mather, Hawthorne, and the latter's descendants, while the Romantic "noble savage," whose idealized life and death is a source of transcendence, can be seen from Neal and Cooper in the 1820s to the "Indian guides" of the Spiritualist mediums and today's New Age believers. Goddu argues for the centrality in American Gothic of Indians as hero-villains and the frontier as Gothic landscape, even though "once assets of America's literary nationalism, the Indian and the gothic" fall out "of a more established canon. Yet as American literature's unacknowledged origins, the gothic and the Indian continue to be hauntingly present" (72). Guilt over slavery may be less obvious, but fear of the Black Man can be traced from Cotton Mather through Melville to the present.

Another Gothic legacy is that of xenophobia and "racial science." Nell Irvin Painter's *The History of White People* traces the expanding definitions of Whiteness in America from its origins to the present. She argues that for White supremacists, "the idea of New England [...] played a pivotal role in American race thought. Ostensibly a regional identity, New England stood for racial Englishness" (207). New England's intellectuals saw their own class as more English than the English. Following the example of Thomas Jefferson, who referred often to "our Saxon ancestors," Emerson embraced the myth of the noble Anglo-Saxon: in his famous essay on "Self-Reliance" (1841), he resembles a twenty-first-century Aryan nationalist, calling on his readers to "wake Thor and Woden, courage and constancy, in our Saxon breasts" (102). Two years later, George Perkins Marsh, a pioneering conservationist, addressed Middlebury College on "The Goths in New England." Marsh is proud that New England has preserved the ideals and ideology of the Puritans

---

3. "Folk horror" describes contemporary fiction and films based in regional legends. A frequent trope is the survival of ancient beliefs, often involving human sacrifice, as in Shirley Jackson's "The Lottery" (1948), whose early readers assumed the practice survived in New England. See Murphy, "The People."

as well as their racial purity, unlike the mongrelized population of "commercial towns" such as New York (39). Marsh's argument relies on the "Gothic myth" in English Whig politics, a belief that the Germanic tribes called "the Goths" were the originators of liberty and democracy, and that these tribes did not destroy Rome—they saved it from absolutism and mystery cults.

The nineteenth century saw a movement to link New England more firmly with Nordic heritage through the search for Leif Erikson's Vinland the Good, which they located in Massachusetts or Maine. Others went even further back to *Eirik the Red's Saga* of a legendary "Hvitramannaland" or "Whiteman's Land": "They said that kings ruled over the land of the Skroelingar [identified with the Indians]. [...] This was supposed to be Hvitramannaland" (Sephton 32). Another translator of the Norse Sagas and proponent of the Vikings as the first settlers of New England was Henry Wadsworth Longfellow. His poem "The Skeleton in Armor" (1843) imagines a history for a skeleton unearthed in Fall River, ascribing the metal "armor" found upon it to Viking builders of Newport's mysterious "Old Stone Mill." Another Harvard professor, Eben Horsford, built a Gothic tower at the head of the Charles River, the site he chose for the lost city of Norumbega, whose name he identified with Norway.[4]

These proponents of fantastic archaeology were supported by the new "American School" of anthropology, which promoted theories of racial hierarchies and the innate inferiority of the Black race from the mid-nineteenth century until they were supplanted by the cultural anthropologists Franz Boas, Ruth Benedict, and Margaret Mead. In the twentieth century, New Englanders embraced the "racial science" of eugenics and used it to support limits on immigration from non-Nordic countries. These anxieties can be found in literature from Charlotte Perkins Gilman through Lovecraft and other Gothic science fiction writers.

From its origins, the Gothic has been considered a disposable genre, caricatured by Jane Austen in *Northanger Abbey* as "the horridest nonsense you can imagine," published as penny dreadfuls, pulp fiction, and paperback best sellers, all deemed unworthy of critical attention. Nevertheless, influential critics, including Leslie Fiedler in *Love and Death in the American Novel* (1960), convinced a new generation that the Gothic mode was central to the canonical figures of American literature. Fiedler's psychological approach to the Gothic can still be found, with critics drawing upon the work of Julia Kristeva, who in *The Powers of Horror* amplified Freud's theory of abjection in literature and life: "It is thus not lack of cleanliness or health that causes abjection but what disturbs identity, system, order. What does not respect borders, positions, rules.

---

4. The derelict tower stands in Waltham, Massachusetts, an object of legend trips and Gothic tourism.

The in-between, the ambiguous, the composite" (4). Like abjection, the composite Gothic resists definition: is it literary genre, mode of thought, or way of life? While providing "A Transnational Perspective on American Gothic Criticism," Sian Silyn Roberts surveys five decades of criticism reacting to Fiedler. Her definition of "Gothic" adds more ambiguity, applying the term "to a body of works, a historical period, a formal aesthetics, a discursive field, and an epistemological theory" (21).

Despite its boundary-crossing nature, the Gothic has most often been studied as a national phenomenon: though the present work focuses on one region of one country, the texts and tropes are not so confined. In the preface to *Tales of the Grotesque and Arabesque* (1840), Poe defines the boundless and limitless nature and the appeal of the Gothic mode: "If in many of my productions terror has been the thesis, I maintain that terror is not of Germany, but of the soul" (6). Born in Boston, Poe spent his life outside of New England, but the influence of his "terror thesis" can be traced in New England writers from his day to the present.

In 2009, the journal *Gothic Studies* observed its 10th anniversary with an issue surveying the Gothic and Theory. The editors noted that critics have viewed the Gothic through the lenses of "revisionist psychoanalysis and Marxism, feminism and gender studies, post-structural deconstruction, 'new' historicism and cultural studies […] queer theory, critical race studies, postcolonial criticism" (Hogle and Smith 1). Since 2009, theories of ecocriticism and posthumanism have also been applied to the Gothic. The Australian critic Helen Young in *Race and Popular Fantasy Literature: Habits of Whiteness* (2015) applies the ethnographic methodology of fan and reception studies along with critical race theory, feminist, and queer theory to contemporary neo-medieval high fantasy. Young's thesis is that fantasy literature and the films and games derived from it construct "the Self through Whiteness and Otherness through […] racist stereotypes, particularly but not exclusively those associated with Blackness" (*Race* 11) and that the consumers of these genres are still dealing with "habits of Whiteness," even though some of the genre's writers may be "struggling to break them" (*Race* 10). These arguments work equally well for the Gothic, the ancestor of today's publishing categories of romance, fantasy, and horror. Young's "habits of whiteness" that we have found in New England's Gothic history include xenophobia against new arrivals and persecution of those already here. As Painter notes, "Hatred of black people did not preclude hatred of other white people—those considered different and inferior" (132). Puritans hanged Quakers as well as witches and (except in Roger Williams's breakaway colony of Rhode Island) excluded Jews from their "New Israel."

My approach to the Gothic belongs under the sign of "Cultural Studies" with its cross-disciplinary emphasis on revealing the secrets of genocide of the native peoples and the African presence/absence. Hogle identifies the "Americanized version" of Britain's Cultural Studies as "pulling together *many* theories" (13; emphasis in original) and studying "relationships between symbolic performances typed as 'high' or dominant culture and [...] 'low' or subaltern culture" (13). I include texts—written and visual—that in the past would not have been taken seriously, for as William Patrick Day writes of his study of the Gothic, "the imaginative life of a culture is not necessarily fully embodied, or most intensely and significantly expressed, in socially acceptable forms" (10). Many of the texts studied here, though written by White Euro-Americans, fit Kathleen Brogan's definition of "cultural haunting." Unlike other ghost stories, concerned primarily with an individual's haunted mind, cultural haunting represents "a people's historical consciousness" and allows the writer to investigate "history through supernatural means" ("American"; *Cultural Haunting*).

The "high" and "low" literature of the American Gothic form a secret history, the perfect site for investigating the politics of the Gothic mode: Is it subversive, undermining received history and consensus reality, or revanchist, looking backward nostalgically and reacting against challenges to Western hegemony? New England's secret history of Puritan hypocrisy, persecution of Quakers and witches, and the long fall from grace is revealed in Hawthorne, King, and Lovecraft, whose tales encode anxieties over slavery, inbreeding, and miscegenation. Another master theme of the secret history, "unholy survivals" of ancient practices, can be seen in the New England vampire belief and in novels and films of Old World cults surviving in the New.

It is a truism that there exist two plots for all literature, from *The Odyssey* (which features both) to the present: someone leaves home, and a stranger comes to town. In the Gothic mode, the two plots could be expressed as "I'm afraid that there's something in my house (*my head*)" and "You're afraid that I have entered your house (*your country*) when I don't belong there." White nationalist and President of MIT Francis A. Walker uses this analogy in "Immigration and Degradation" (1891). Walker compares a New England village where "the house had been kept in order" but was now occupied by immigrants' "houses that were mere shells for human habitations, the gate unhung, the shutters flapping" (640–41) to the inevitable destruction of American society by foreigners who were replacing and outbreeding the native stock. In his New England, colonial houses are haunted by immigrant demons.

The monsters may be inside us or outsiders, but either way, they haunt us. Named by Jeffrey Jerome Cohen in 1996, his "Seven Theses" toward a Monster Theory generated a flood of scholarship that like his monsters defied category and disciplinary boundaries.[5] The monstrous in literature and in life is simultaneously feared and desired. The monster is a representation of difference—Cohen's "Thesis IV: The Monster Dwells at the Gates of Difference" (7). The supernatural monster can be read as a (*subject*) projection of our fears of difference in race, religion, gender, or bodily form, while humans of different races, religions, genders, or bodily forms may be transformed (*objects*) into monsters. In *Black Looks: Race and Representation* (1992), feminist and critical race theorist bell hooks examines this fear of and desire for the Other in film, literature, and life, "suggesting alternative ways to look at blackness, black subjectivity, and, of necessity, whiteness" (5).[6]

Learning about a culture by studying what it finds monstrous maps neatly onto the Mathers' project of collecting horrifying wonders. Cotton Mather was aware of the dangers involved. After a horrific depiction in *Magnalia Christi Americana* (1702) of monstrous births to the heretical feminist preacher Anne Hutchinson, he notes that "my study where I was writing, and the chamber where my wife was sitting, shook, as we thought, with an earthquake, by the space of half a quarter of an hour. We both perceived it. [...] My wife said it was the devil that was displeased that we confer about this occasion" (449). Hutchinson's monster baby was buried "without any noise of its monstrosity," but "the magistrates ordered the opening of the grave," and the secret was revealed (2: 449). In accord with Monster Theory, Mather felt a "simultaneous repulsion and attraction" (Cohen 17) to Hutchinson's story. Despite his wife's warning, Mather would continue chronicling Satan's business with New England, just as he would answer those who criticized his support for and pursuit of the Salem witch trials by saying that to deny the reality of Satan was to deny the existence of God.

---

5. Jeffrey Weinstock's *The Monster Theory Reader* (2020) reprints Cohen's "Seven Theses" and more recent scholarship on the monstrous.
6. Gloria Watkins chose this pen name to honor her great-grandmother, using lower case to emphasize ideas rather than authorship.

Chapter 2

THE PURITANS' HAUNTED FRONTIER

It was not long before the Hand which now writes, upon a certain occasion took off the *jaw* from the blasphemous exposed *Skull* of that *Leviathan.*

— Cotton Mather, *The Triumphs of the Reformed Religion*
(1691); emphasis in original

The Wampanoag chieftain Metacomet, known as King Philip, led a confederation of tribes against the English colonists in 1675–76. Captured, he was punished as a traitor would have been in England, as Increase Mather describes: "cut into four quarters, [...] hanged up as a monument of revenging Justice, his head being cut off and carried away to Plymouth, his Hands were brought to Boston" (*A Brief* 72). Philip's head presided over a day of "publick Thanksgiving" in Plymouth on August 17, 1676. In Mather's words: "God [...] delivered Philip into their hands a few dayes before their intended Thanksgiving. Thus did God break the head of that Leviathan, and gave it to be meat to the people inhabiting the wilderness, and brought it to the Town of Plimouth the very day of their solemn Festival" (*A Brief* 73). This Thanksgiving is *not* commemorated in modern Plymouth. A few years later, Reverend Mather brought his son, Cotton, to view the head. The boy ripped the jawbone from King Philip's skull and kept it as a souvenir (*Triumphs* 107). Robert Lowell may be alluding to this event as well as to John the Baptist in his poem "At the Indian Killer's Grave": "Philip's head / Grins on the platter" (56) and again in his sonnet "Concord": "The death-dance of King Philip and his scream / Whose echo girdled this imperfect globe" (1946: 27).

The fate of King Philip's head demonstrates several themes of the New England Frontier Gothic to be examined in this chapter: Puritan visions of apocalypse; fear of organized attack by the indigenous peoples who are seen as monsters in life and after death; and later writers' nostalgia for the "last of" their race or guilt over their extinction. Puritan fears of attack by Satanic forces are also evident in accounts of witch trials and demonic possession, which became taproot texts for centuries of New England's Gothic literature.

Apocalypticism

> Oh fearful Doom! now there's no room for hope or help at all.
> —Wigglesworth, *The Day of Doom* (1662)

The Puritan worldview expressed itself in utopian and dystopian visions, both of which characterize American literature writ large as well as the New England Gothic. The Bible's Book of Revelations, source for Michael Wigglesworth's popular poem *The Day of Doom* (1662), provides vivid imagery of the Last Judgment, following upon visitations of war, famine, plague, and violent death—the Four Horsemen. Fearing God's judgment on sinners and believing in original sin, Puritans might well be pessimistic about the end of their lives' journey. The doctrine of predestination meant constant anxiety over whether one would be part of the elect. At the same time, believers were dedicated to bringing God's Kingdom to Earth through building new communities, giving us the Plymouth Colony's "we were Pilgrims" and John Winthrop's vision of Boston as the biblical City on a Hill.

The terrors of an inevitable harsh judgment inspired the Gothic Puritan apocalypticism expressed in the jeremiad or political sermon. Increase Mather's famed sermon on King Philip's War characterized it as punishment for backsliding New England "Saints" as well as a portent of apocalypse: "the Calamity which is come upon New-England, is a solemn warning from Heaven, that dismal things are hastening upon the English Nation, and not only so, but indeed upon the whole World" ("Earnest" 33).

The same imagery can be found in later religious revivals, most notably in Jonathan Edwards's "Sinners in the Hands of an Angry God" (1741). This sermon inspires nightmares to this day, with its God who "abhors" the sinner, holding him over the Pit of Hell, "as one holds a Spider or some lothsom Insect over the Fire" (16). Edwards addresses his listeners intimately, reminding them of that slender, singed thread in God's hand, "and nothing to lay hold of to save yourself, [...] nothing you ever have done, nothing that you can do, to induce God to spare you one Moment" (17). Edwards's sermon apparently inspired one member of his flock to commit suicide. *Spider in a Tree* (2013) by Susan Stinson, a resident of Northampton, Massachusetts, site of Edwards's church, imagines the minister's tormented life as well as those of the slaves in his household.

The hope of establishing God's kingdom on Earth may have led to the utopian experiment that is the United States of America, whose constitution declares its purpose as "to form a more perfect Union." Prosaically, this could refer to the inadequacy of the prior Articles of Confederation, but the search for an ideal Commonwealth in American culture looks backward toward

Winthrop's City on a Hill and forward to hundreds of years of intentional communities both religious and secular.

The two peaks of commune building in New England—attempts at bringing Eden to Earth—are the 1840s and the 1960s. The unsuccessful Brook Farm and Fruitlands communities of the transcendentalists have been immortalized in Louisa May Alcott's satirical "Transcendental Wild Oats" and in a more Gothic fashion in Hawthorne's *The Blithedale Romance*. Another transcendentalist commune of the 1840s, the Northampton Association of Education and Industry, successfully ran a silk mill. This rare interracial experiment included Sojourner Truth and David Ruggles as members. They were dedicated to establishing a utopian society "that shall Substitute Fraternal Co-operation for Antagonistic Selfishness; a Religious Consecration of Life and Labor, Soul and Body, Time and Eternity" (qtd. in Ballou 132).[1] Though transcendentalist philosophy and utopian dreams may seem the opposite of the Gothic mode, this may be a case of *coincidentia oppositorum*. The Gothic has room for extremes of optimism and idealism as well as for depression and despair at the human condition. In "Descendentalism and the Dark Romantics: Poe, Hawthorne, Melville and the Subversion of American Transcendentalism," Ted Billy claims that the relationship of these writers to the transcendentalism of Emerson and Thoreau is a reexamination on both sides of the oppositions of man/nature and civilization/wilderness. The search for transcendence can be found in the late eighteenth-century concept of the Gothic sublime as well as in Swedenborg or Emerson.

There is something in the Gothic that leads to world-explaining secret histories and philosophies. This strain of the Gothic proposes that the world is not as we think it to be. As Poe wrote: "All that we see or seem/Is but a dream within a dream," or more often a nightmare of a world run by a malevolent conspiracy whose existence is revealed only to poets and dreamers. All can be explained by the Illuminati or the Elder Gods or the Knights Templar or the Elders of Zion. Poe's treatise as prose-poem *Eureka* is one such system. Succeeding attempts at explaining the universe as a forbidden text include Lovecraft's "cosmic indifferentism" or "weird materialism." In fiction, the apocalyptic combination of shadow governments, cultists, sorcerers, and monsters is a potent one: exemplified in Lovecraft, it can be found in Caitlin Kiernan's "Black Helicopters" series and in other responses to Lovecraft by Ruthanna Emrys and Douglas Wynne, to be discussed in Chapter 4.

---

1. Adin Ballou founded Hopedale, another intentional community. He was the cousin of Major Sullivan Ballou, author of the letter to Sarah featured in Ken Burns's documentary *Civil War*.

Indian Wars

> And the bones and skulls upon the several places of their habitations
> made such a spectacle after my coming into those partes, that, as I
> travailed in that Forrest nere the Massachusetts it seemed to mee a new
> found Golgotha.
>
> —Thomas Morton, *The New English Canaan* (1637)

King Philip's War was neither the first nor the last armed encounter between
the English colonists and the native peoples of New England. The earliest
and most deadly battle, however, was fought with microbes. Earlier European
explorers and fishermen had brought clear-field epidemics to the shores of
Massachusetts, resulting in the Pilgrims' discovery that (in their view) God
had cleared the land of its inhabitants. Writing in 1654, Edward Johnson
concludes that "by this meanes Christ [...] not onely made roome for his
people to plant; but also tamed the hard and cruell hearts of these barbarous
Indians" (41). Among the tribes who suffered from the great pestilence were
"the Pecods," "who retained the Name of a war-like people, till afterwards
conquered by the English" (41). Recounting his victory in the Pequot War of
1637, Connecticut's Captain John Mason saw God's hand in his burning of
their fort, "who laughed his Enemies and the Enemies of his People to Scorn,
making them as a fiery Oven. [...] Thus did the LORD judge among the
Heathen, filling the Place with dead Bodies!" (9). The poet Lydia Sigourney
in an essay "The Fall of the Pequod" (1846) takes a different view of the
events: she chides Mason for "kindling the flame over the heads of slum-
bering households and smiting the infant in its mother's arms" (138). The
Pequot War ended with survivors being exiled or sold into slavery, the earliest
recorded enslavement in the Northern colonies.

Almost four decades after New Englanders celebrated that victory, King
Philip's War was traumatic for the Puritans. Jill Lepore's *The Name of War*
(1998) credits this conflict with forming American identity. She theorizes that
Cotton Mather took the jawbone to symbolically "silence" King Philip (174–
75). Perhaps in Gothic fashion, Mather was preventing this monster whom he
and his father compared to the Apocalyptic beast Leviathan from telling the
true story. Washington Irving's essay on "Philip of Pokanoket" in his *Sketch
Book* (1820) presents the Gothic legends that grew up about King Philip:

> He was an evil that walked in darkness. [...] Many superstitious notions
> were circulated concerning him. He was said to deal in necromancy
> and to be attended by an old Indian witch, or prophetess, whom he
> consulted and who assisted him by her charms and incantations. This

indeed was frequently the case [...] and the influence of the prophet and the dreamer over Indian superstition has been fully evidenced in recent instances of savage warfare. (256–57)

Though Metacomet's attempt to unite the native peoples failed, individual tribes continued to resist the English colonists. More conflicts followed in the 1680s; these and attacks on York, Maine, in 1691–92 have been linked with the witch panic in Salem. By the American Revolution, these wars were a distant memory, and the frontier had moved far from New England. Nevertheless, ghosts of the Indians dead from plague and war continued to haunt the victors. Colleen Boyd and Coll Thrush in *Phantom Past, Indigenous Presence* (2011) spell out the role of native ghosts in the North American imagination and the cultural significance of this haunting:

Native ghosts—whether in print or on screen [...] express the moral anxieties and uncertainties provoked by the dispossession of a place's Indigenous inhabitants. [...] Native hauntings disrupt dominant and official historical narratives as expressions of liminality that transcend fixed boundaries of time and space. (ix)

As we will see, memories of New England's original inhabitants are preserved as ghosts in Gothic literature and film, though their living descendants may be ignored or forgotten.

The Frontier Gothic on Land and Sea

The Indian is the only native American [...] the Americans, their brothers are thinning them day after day like a pestilence [...] pushing them from the tombs of their ancestors.

—John Neal, *Keep Cool* (1817)

Colonists who were captured during the Indian wars of the seventeenth century and survived were the subjects or authors of captivity narratives, taproot texts for Frontier Gothic fiction. Like other providence tales, Indian captivity narratives demonstrate God's power through depiction of horrors and wonders. The most famous North American captive in the colonial period, Mary Rowlandson (1682) relayed her experience during King Philip's War in terms familiar to later readers of Gothic horror: describing the initial attack, "like a company of sheep torn by wolves, all of them stripped naked by a company of hell-hounds," and the next day, "oh the roaring, and singing and dancing, and yelling of those black creatures in the night, which made the place a lively resemblance of hell" (Rowlandson 1675). Mather and Rowlandson consistently portray the Indian captors as Gothic villains who gloat over helpless females or as wild animals such as wolves and bears. Though the surviving captives did not mention cannibalism or human sacrifice, the belief persisted that the Indians followed these practices, as Scottow reports (1694), calling them "Cruel Cannibals, Scalping and Fleaing of our Bodies, burning us as Sacrifices to Habamoch [Hobomock]" (41).

Rowlandson attempted to assuage her captors, sewing for them in exchange for food; Hannah Dustan took the opposite tack. Taken captive along with the midwife who had attended her a week earlier and her infant murdered, she and the nurse killed and scalped their Indian captors with their own hatchets. Cotton Mather narrates Hannah Dustan's exploits in *Decennium Luctuosum* (1699) and in *Magnalia Christi*. He justifies Dustan's actions because she lived on the lawless frontier and praises her by evoking the biblical heroine Jael, who killed her opponent with a tent peg through the head. Rowlandson's narrative continued to inspire writers of New England Frontier Gothic: her Hell-hound Indian captors appear in Harriet Beecher Stowe's *Oldtown Fireside Story*, "Colonel Eph's Shoe-Buckles" (1872).

As early as 1817, John Neal argues for the Indian cause and laments their treatment in America. Melodramatic action scenes join moments of the Gothic sublime in the wilderness in his first published work *Keep Cool*, anticipating by a decade James Fenimore Cooper's more famous *The Last of the Mohicans*. Nathaniel Hawthorne's "Roger Malvin's Burial" (1832) portrays other dangers of the wilderness in a tale of curse and expiation on the Maine frontier, a battle in 1725 that he terms "Lovell's Fight" (88).[2] Hawthorne's protagonist fails to carry out his vow to the dying Malvin and leaves his bones unburied in the "howling wilderness." The story focuses not on the Indians but on how Reuben's life is blighted and haunted by "the secret effect of guilt" (175). This miniature Greek tragedy ends with the cursed Reuben accidentally shooting his only son at the very rock where he had abandoned his wife's father, Roger Malvin. Hawthorne's favorite theme of guilt "like a serpent gnawing into his heart" (176) can also be found in both Hester and Dimmesdale in *The Scarlet Letter* (1850); in the allegory "Egotism; or, the Bosom Serpent" (1843); and in "Ethan Brand" (1851), whose title character searches the world for "the Unpardonable Sin" and finds it in his own heart.

Harriet Prescott Spofford's bloodcurdling Frontier Gothic story "Circumstance" was originally published serially in the *Atlantic* (1860),

---

2. For colonial ballads about "Lovewell" and the Indians, see Gray (127–39).

whose editor did not believe it could have been the work of a 25-year-old woman. Emily Dickinson praised the powerful story to her sister-in-law, Susan Huntington Dickinson, as "the only thing that I ever saw in my life that I did not think I could have written myself" (qtd. in Weinstock, *Scare* 29n7). Spofford claimed the events of the story had happened to her great-grandmother in the Maine wilderness. The villain of the story, however, is not an Indian but "the Indian Devil"—a panther. The language used to describe the beast is that of the Gothic seducer: "holding her in his great lithe embrace [...] his eyes glaring through all the darkness like balls of red fire" (158). The beast's rough tongue licks the heroine's arm, but she saves herself: "She had heard that music charmed wild beasts" (158), and throughout the winter's night in a tree in the wilderness, she sings for her life. Her husband finally tracks her and shoots the panther, whose body breaks her fall and she survives, but the Frontier Gothic has one more blow. When husband, wife, and baby reach their cabin, "there is no home there [...] all blotted out and mingled in one smoking ruin. [...] Tomahawk and scalping-knife, descending during that night, had left behind them only this work of their accomplished hatred" (172).

Another example of New England's Frontier Gothic, also written by a young woman, is Lydia Maria Child's *Hobomok* (1824). Child's daring first novel presents an interracial marriage in which the woman takes the lead: "Child makes the link between marriage and death explicit by having [Mary] Conant propose to Hobomok while standing on her mother's grave. [...] She is an outcast, a sexually transgressive specter like Hester Prynne" (Bergland 75). We are reminded of Mary and Percy Shelley's legendary tryst on her mother's tomb. Earlier in the story, the narrator sees Conant engaged in a ritual at her mother's grave, "childish witchery" that he compares with the "inward warfare" of his own mind (Child, *Hobomok* chap. 1). *Hobomok*'s title character is named for a deity and culture hero identified by Puritans with Satan.[3] Mary weds Hobomok when she hears that her English lover has died at sea. The novel's ending, however, is more sentimental than Gothic: the lost lover is found, and the noble Hobomok disappears to make way for him. Child portrays Indian customs and religion sympathetically, along with the intolerant obduracy of the Puritans. Child is more famous today for her abolitionist activities, including *An Appeal in Favor of That Class of Americans Called Africans* (1833). She also edited and obtained a publisher for Harriet Jacobs's slave narrative.

Another early writer of New England romances, Catherine Maria Sedgwick, comes from the distinguished family in Stockbridge, Massachusetts,

---

3. See Scottow (41); Ringel (*New* 56–57).

currently represented by actress Kyra Sedgwick. *A New-England Tale* (1822) is a transplanted sentimental novel that also shows signs of its author's immersion in the first Gothic revival. The caddish suitor vows, "I shall never addict myself to divinity, till Anne Ratcliffe [*sic*] writes sermons" (114). A major intrusion of the Gothic is the character of Crazy Bet, a Massachusetts version of Madge Wildfire from Walter Scott's *Heart of Midlothian* who leads the protagonist into the dangerous wilderness.

Frontier Gothic may also embrace the trope of the noble savage, the Romantic movement's ideal of the innate goodness of primitive humanity before the corruption of civilization. These authors blame Europeans for introducing vices such as intemperance and greed so that the remaining "savages" of their time have fallen from that uncorrupted state. Early American poet Philip Freneau's "The Indian Burying-Ground" (1787) mingles the Gothic melancholy of the English Graveyard School with a lament for a vanishing race. Encountering the Indian ghosts, "the hunter and the deer, a shade!" the poet reminds onlookers that "reason's self shall bow the knee / To shadows and delusions here" (369–70). In the nineteenth century, poets, journalists, and novelists eulogized "the last of ..." various native tribes. In 1834, Lydia Sigourney wrote a poem for the dedication of the Mohegan Congregational Church in eastern Connecticut, expressing sorrow for the treatment of the Mohegan tribe and all Indians. She evokes the blood-soaked battleground upon which the church stands: "Now where tradition, ghostly pale, / With ancient horrors loads the vale, / And shuddering weaves, in crimson loom/ Ambush, and snare, and torture-doom." She marvels at the tribal members' restraint and Christian spirit while lamenting the end of their noble line:

> —Crush'd race!—so long condemned to moan,
> Scorn'd—rifled—spiritless—and lone,
> From pagan rites, from sorrow's maze,
> Turn to these temple-gates with praise;
> Yes, turn and bless the usurping band
> That rent away your fathers' land.
>
> (Sigourney, *Selected Poems* 325)

Such "Last of ..." laments ignored the continued existence of the Indians they memorialized. Jean O'Brien's study of nineteenth-century local histories saw town historians "literally refusing to recognize New England Indians as 'authentic' Indians" (428) since they had engaged in racial mixing with Black people and were no longer "pure-blooded" and because they no longer practiced traditional Indian ways. As late as 1869, Harriet Beecher Stowe can have the narrator of *Oldtown Folks* observe of John Eliot, the seventeenth-century

"Apostle to the Indians": "He taught them agriculture, and many of the arts and trades of civilized life. But he could not avert the doom which seems to foreordain that those races shall dry up and pass away with their native forests" (3)—as though European colonization had nothing to do with this "doom" of extinction.

Indians may have appeared more suitable for romantic musings once they were dead or removed from New England, but the motif of the "Indian curse" on their conquerors passed into Gothic legend. In 1936, Princess Red Wing of the Narragansetts in Rhode Island transmitted this story from King Philip's War:

> That each of those spruce trees grow where a drop of Narragansett blood was shed. They will ever grow in South County, no matter how much civilization crowds them. It is said of one settler, that he decided to cut down every spruce on his 500 acres of Indian land because they haunted him, and he was killed in the attempt. (qtd. in Simmons 142)

Cultural anthropologist Simmons notes that the transformation of dead men into trees appears in the mythology of several Indian nations. In *Memory Lands: King Philip's War and the Place of Violence in the Northeast*, Christine DeLucia comments that "the very trees reproached non-Natives, reminding them of the dispossession and violence underlying contemporary claims to private property" (174). Another legend still circulating in oral tradition among the Mashantucket Pequots attributes the bright crimson centers of rhododendrons that grow in mast swamp on the reservation (now home to Foxwoods Casino) to the Pequot blood shed there in 1637.[4] The legend states that survivors of the massacre of the Pequot fort had sought refuge in the swamp, where they starved and were captured and drowned or sold into slavery. The chief, Putaquaponk, was captured in the swamp, where he "cursed the English for their craving for human blood. He prophesied that the flowers which nodded in the breeze above him would show golden hearts no longer, but hearts of blood instead, as a reproach to the white people" (Skinner 131).

Nor were Indians the only marginalized group who laid curses: another eastern Connecticut story tells of the persecution of a Quaker offshoot group known as the Rogerenes who refused to recognize congregationalist authority, the established church in Connecticut until 1818. In 1726, some Rogerenes were sentenced to be publicly whipped for their defiance with branches of the

---

4. See Simmons; Skinner; Citro, *Cursed in New England*.

"prim" bush (whose flower is the primrose), and they cursed the shrub, which eventually withered (Caulkins 350).

The Frontier Gothic in its modern iteration includes the dangerous humans to be found in the wilderness suffering the effects of isolation. This aspect of Frontier Gothic is more often associated with the haunted wilderness of Canada or the brutal Outback of Australia. In American Frontier Gothic, narratives of cabin fever lead to madness, as Edith Wharton writes, "It's a worm in the brain, solitude is" ("Bewitched"). Stories of men killing their families are referred to by natives and Euro-Americans as "going Wendigo." The Wendigo is the wilderness personified as a spirit that brings cold in its wake, that can possess or madden human intruders and turn them into cannibals. In *Pet Sematary*, Stephen King blames the Wendigo for the necromantic horrors of his desecrated native burial ground. King calls it "the Wendigo, creature of the north country, the dead thing whose touch awakens unspeakable appetites" (363). Citro's *The Unseen* (1987) also draws on legends of the Wendigo. As a former logger declares, "any man who wintered in the loggin' camps knows about the winny-go" (140). The novel is set in one of Vermont's gores, liminal spaces in the contemporary frontier known as the Northeast Kingdom. The Wendigo monster, however, is a modern addition to New England lore. Not found in legends of its native tribes, the Wendigo haunts the Cree and Ojibwa in the United States and other First Peoples in Canada.[5]

Northern New England's landscape reminds artist and Vermont Gothic scholar Steve Bissette of the Scandinavian settings of the Bergman films he watched while growing up: "The tree line and the sky like a bowl above our heads creates a feeling of isolation." His friend and collaborator Joe Citro agrees: "The landscape and personality of Vermont play as much of a role in my books as character or plot." Horror novelist Rick Hautala found resonance between the landscape and myths of his Finnish ancestors and the native legends and landscapes of his home state of Maine. *Untcigahunk—the Complete Little Brothers* (2012) collects Hautala's novel and short stories, which transform Algonquian beliefs about nature spirits or "little people" into small, vicious monsters, who emerge periodically to revenge themselves upon today's Mainers. Commonalities between the cultures do exist in shamanic traditions: Longfellow made that connection explicit by modeling *The Song of Hiawatha* (1856), his Native American epic, on the meter and legends of the *Kalevala*, Finland's national epic poem. In late twentieth-century horror fiction and film, the repressed return with a vengeance when suburban houses are built over Indian burial grounds—most famously in the films *Poltergeist* (1982)

---

5. For indigenous writers such as Louise Erdrich who use the Wendigo belief in their Gothic fiction, see Brogan, "American"; Burnham.

and *The Amityville Horror* (1979). In New England, this trope of the desecrated Indian burial ground was popularized in Stephen King's *Pet Sematary* (1983) and its film adaptations.

Fear of the forest was matched by fear of the haunted ocean, ecophobia of another type of wilderness. The dangers of the unknowable depths were personified in Early Modern Europe by sea monsters, and explorers of seventeenth-century New England brought those beliefs with them. The biblical Leviathan was never far from their minds, as Melville shows us in *Moby-Dick*, whose "Leviathan comes floundering down upon us from the head-waters of the Eternities" (510). English explorer John Josselyn on his 1639 voyage just missed seeing a sea serpent, "quoiled up like a Cable upon a Rock at Cape-Ann" (22). Thoreau's *Journal* recounts Daniel Webster's voyage in quest of a similar serpent off Massachusetts's south coast. Stephen Vincent Benét's tall tale "Daniel Webster and the Sea Serpent" (1937) endows the embodiment of Leviathan with the personality of a New England spinster who falls in love with Senator Webster.

Belief in sea serpents and lake monsters persists. Josselyn's sea serpent of Cape Ann continues to be sighted: F. Brett Cox juxtaposes this bit of Gothic maritime legend with the temperance crusaders of Rockport, Massachusetts, in "The Serpent and the Hatchet Gang" (2007). Citro's novel *Dark Twilight* assumes that the monster once sighted by the explorer Samuel de Champlain may still be found in the lake that bears his name. "Champ," star of TV and tabloids, is a friendly Vermont tourist attraction. Citro's vision is more Gothic: "a dark, serpentine form" that "roved silently through shadowless depths" (211); in addition to "Champ," the novel's characters encounter even more frightening monsters on an island in the lake. Two other glacial lakes in Vermont have monster legends: Willoughby and Memphremagog, whose lake serpent is called "Memphré." The fear of dragons in the deep still haunts New England's lake and seashores.

Another hazard of navigation was the sighting of a ghost ship. A particularly well-attested one sailed in the sky above the harbor in New Haven, Connecticut, in 1647. Originally reported in *Winthrop's Journal* (2: 346), the story can be heard today. Longfellow's poem "The Phantom Ship" (1850) recounts the apparition of a "Ship of Air" (*Poems* 327) based on Mather's version in *Magnalia Christi*.[6] Mather addresses us directly: "Reader, there being yet living so many credible gentlemen, that were eye-witnesses of this wonderful thing, I venture to publish it for a thing as undoubted as 'tis wonderful" (1: 84).

Like Mather, New Hampshire's John Greenleaf Whittier collected the supernatural legends of his native land; unlike his predecessor, he transformed them into verse. Whittier's ballad of the "Dead Ship of Harpswell" preserves

---

6. See also E. Mitchell, "The Legendary Ship."

coastal Maine folklore; Whittier provides a more hopeful ending for those who
see this portent of death:

> They know not that its sails are filled
> > By pity's tender breath,
> Nor see the Angel at the helm
> > Who steers the Ship of Death!
>
> > > > > (Whittier, *Poems* 63)

The same ghost ship features in Robert P. Tristram Coffin's novel *John Dawn*
(1936). This historical Gothic with an element of time travel features a "Dead
Ship" called the *Harpswell,* which for the novel's narrator and characters is
a harbinger of death. Whittier also immortalized the *Palatine,* a ghost ship
whose fiery wreck is still reported off Block Island. In Whittier's version, the
islanders are cursed for their actions of luring the ship on the rocks, looting it,
and setting it afire:

> In their cruel hearts, as they homeward sped,
> "The sea and the rocks are dumb," they said:
> "There'll be no reckoning with the dead."
>
> > > > > (*Poems* 257–58).

Today's Block Islanders tell a different story, blaming Whittier for slandering
their ancestors. Folklorist Michael Bell has collected accounts of the "Palatine
light" appearing on the anniversary of its wreck in late December 1738 ("The
Legend").

The ultimate Gothic ghost ship must be the *Mystery.*

> She was a slave-ship long ago.
> > Year after year across the sea
> She made a trade of human woe,
> > And carried freights of misery.
>
> > > > > (Thaxter 6)

Celia Thaxter, poet, gardener, and chronicler of the legends of New
Hampshire's coastal Isles of Shoals, created this poem, "The Cruise of the
Mystery" (1886), about a slaver captain who dumps his dead cargo overboard.
They return to wreak revenge on the captain and crew. The resulting ghost
ship is a harbinger of death to those who see her—and another return of the
repressed.

The Witch Belief and Its Consequences

> But as for us *Nov-Angli*, New English, by our smutty deformity, and Hells
> blackness, we have rendred ourselves *Diaboli Veterans*, Old Devils: *New*
> *England* will be called, new Witch-land.
>
> —Joshua Scottow, *A NARRATIVE of the Planting of the*
> *Massachusets COLONY* (1694); emphasis in original

The witch belief is the best-documented manifestation of New England's
Gothic history because here the supernatural intersected with common law.
Victims of sea serpents, ghosts, or other revenants did not seek justice in the
courts. Those who had grievances such as dying cattle, unexplained human
ailments, and strangely behaving daughters did not hesitate to accuse their
neighbors of malefic witchcraft. It would be impossible to survey here the
330 years of attempts to explain the witch hunts and trials in Massachusetts in
1692–93. That panic swept not only Salem but all of Essex County and nearby
New Hampshire. There was even an "echo panic" in Connecticut's Fairfield
County. Salem Village, locus of the witch hunt, later changed its name to
Danvers to dissociate itself from the judicial murder of 20 innocent people
and others uncounted who died in prison or were forced to flee. There had
been trials for witchcraft in the English colonies before Salem: Connecticut
hanged its first witch in 1639. But only in Salem did clergy and civil government place such trust in the testimony of a group of young women known as
"the afflicted girls," who blamed their affliction on the specters of living men
and women. Based on this "spectral evidence," hundreds were accused of
conspiring with Satan against humanity.[7]

The witch hunts of the seventeenth century are linked to Frontier Gothic
in Cotton Mather's texts that identify Indians with devil worshippers. George
Burroughs, the minister executed as a wizard in Salem, figures as a survivor of Indian attacks in Maine in John Neal's *Rachel Dyer* (1828), a Gothic
romance of the witch trials and the Quaker persecution. This early historical
fiction links the fear of Indian attacks with the fear of witches, as modern
historians have done. Neal may have been inspired by the *Magnalia Christi*,
in which Mather interrupts his account of Satan's siege of Essex County
with "some strange things, not here to be mentioned, have made me often
think, that this inexplicable war might have some of its original among the
Indians" (*Magnalia* 2: 537). Scholars have documented the connection, most

---

7. K. David Goss's *The Salem Witch Trials: A Reference Guide* is a good starting point. Rosenthal
   analyzes the conflicting theories. See also Ringel, *New* 75–135. For documents of the
   witch hunts, see Burr; Hall; Boyer and Nissenbaum.

comprehensively in Mary Beth Norton's *In the Devil's Snare: The Salem Witchcraft Crisis of 1692* (2002).[8]

This eruption of the unexplained Gothic into mundane life haunts the American imagination. Nevertheless, fictional treatments of the witch belief have more often been intended as historical realism, rather than as supernatural Gothic.[9] While Nathaniel Hawthorne, descendant of a witch trial judge, drew on his Puritan family history for his great romances *The Scarlet Letter* and *The House of the Seven Gables* (1851), in neither of these are the witch trials the center of the narrative. The curse that drives the plot of *The House of the Seven Gables* links the work to the European Gothic, where the "witch's curse" had become a cliché. The cursing witch is usually portrayed as a crone, but Hawthorne attributes the curse to the male "Wizard Maule." The wizard curses Colonel Pyncheon and his descendants in the reported words of the condemned witch Sarah Good to Reverend Nicholas Noyes: "'you are a Lyer; I am no more a Witch than you are a Wizard, and if you take away my life, God will give you Blood to drink'" (Burr 358). Thomas Hutchinson (1795)[10] adds a footnote to his account of the fate of Sarah Good: "They have a tradition [...] that a peculiar circumstance attended the death of [Reverend Noyes], he having been choaked with blood, which makes them suppose her, if not a witch, a Pythoniss [*oracular prophet*]" (56n). Hutchinson attributes the story to Calef in *More Wonders of the Invisible World*. Calef's account, printed in London in 1700, is not sympathetic to the conduct of the Mathers in the trials or in the subsequent exorcism of Margaret Rule. Increase Mather ordered the offending book burned in Harvard Yard.

Hawthorne transfers Reverend Noyes's death to the males of the Pyncheon family. *The House of the Seven Gables*, the archetypal haunted house, is erected "over an unquiet grave" of the "dead and buried wizard" (13), a trope found frequently in recent novels and horror films. The novel is linked to Frontier Gothic by Baker and Kences, reflecting actual land speculation on the Maine frontier. A subplot of the novel is the lost Indian land deed granted to Judge Pyncheon. These lands "comprised the greater part of what is now known as Waldo County, in the State of Maine, and were more extensive than many a dukedom" (*House* 22). The family could never claim what they believed was rightfully theirs. Instead, they maintained a map of their purchase, "grotesquely illuminated with the pictures of Indians and wild beasts" (39; Baker

---

8. See also Karlsen; Baker and Kences.
9. See DeRosa on Salem in fiction and drama.
10. Hutchinson was the last royal governor of the "Province" of Massachusetts. His house was invaded during riots following the Stamp Act, destroying materials for the history quoted here.

and Kences 181). The contrivance by which the mystery is solved, hidden behind a portrait with a secret spring, comes straight from the earliest English Gothic romances: Ginsberg argues that this and other parallels with *The Castle of Otranto* make the Puritan haunted house "a fitting symbol for Hawthorne's anxieties over the transatlantic origins of his Gothic house of fiction" (42).

Nathaniel Hawthorne's *Twice-Told Tales* and *Mosses from an Old Manse* collect and transmute the same sorts of wondrous folktales that had fascinated the Mathers. "The Hollow of the Three Hills" is a witch legend set "in those strange old times when fantastic dreams and madmen's reveries were realized among the actual circumstances of life" (191). Hawthorne immortalizes the unorthodox settler Thomas Morton (who pitied the Indians who died in the pestilence) in "The Maypole of Merry Mount." Thomas Morton was no Puritan, though not the pagan high priest of the story, merely a member of the Church of England who did set up a Maypole at his colony "Ma-Re Mount" (today's Quincy, Massachusetts). Morton traded peacefully with the Indians, providing a pretext for the Massachusetts Bay Colony to attack and arrest him. As Hawthorne says, the allegory writes itself. "But what was the wild throng that stood hand in hand about the Maypole? [...] These were Gothic monsters" (50) imported straight from the European Middle Ages. Governor Endicott topples the Maypole and punishes the merry dancers.[11] Hawthorne's *The Blithedale Romance* (1852) has a similar group of costumed revelers celebrating May Day in the woods along with New World characters including a Shaker, Revolutionary War officers, and "a negro of the Jim Crow order" (a White man in blackface) (191).

Hawthorne's "Feathertop: A Moralized Legend" (1854) concerns a scarecrow created and animated by a Salem witch. The legend, entirely Hawthorne's own, is satirical as well as moralizing: "There are thousands upon thousands of coxcombs and charlatans in the world, made up of just such a jumble of wornout, forgotten, and good-for-nothing trash as he was! Yet they live in fair repute, and never see themselves for what they are" (286). *The Scarecrow, or The Glass of Truth: A Tragedy of the Ludicrous* (1908) by Percy MacKaye is not, its author claims, precisely an adaptation of "Feathertop." Besides changing the scarecrow's name to something more menacingly Gothic, MacKaye offers "a divergent treatment and a different conclusion." This "American folk drama" has had many revivals; the most recent adaptation, a made-for-TV movie *The Scarecrow* (1972) starred Gene Wilder as the scarecrow Ravensbane.

---

11. John Beckman's *American Fun* makes Morton of Merry Mount his emblem for chaotic, unruly "fun," symbol of "the New World as an open playground for freedom, equality, and saucy frolic" (5).

Hawthorne incarnates the Gothic in New England, from his earliest sketches to his final unfinished novel *Dr. Grimshawe's Secret* (1882), redacted and completed by his son Julian, an author of fantasy and Gothic romance who served time for fraud.

In *Locke Amsden* (1847) by D. P. Thompson, a New England novelist whose popularity once rivaled Hawthorne's, a schoolteacher in rural Vermont encounters the witch belief that "led us almost to doubt whether we had not [...] been carried back a century and a half, and set down among a clan of the immediate disciples of old Cotton Mather" (100); villagers accused him of knowing too much about mathematics, a short step from magic and devil worship. "Indeed, there was a certain point in figures, they supposed, beyond which, if a person persisted in going, he was sure to have help from one who should be nameless, but who always exacted his pay for his assistance" (99). The schoolmaster is saved from violence by the aptly named Captain Bunker, who debunks the claims of supernatural powers. Thompson also wrote *Lucy Hosmer, or, The Guardian and Ghost* (1848), a novella of Gothic melodrama whose ghost is explained as a trick.

Nineteenth-century poets drew on the witch belief. Lucy Larcom, once a Lowell mill girl, portrayed "Mistress Hale of Beverly," whose husband Reverend Hale had been the most enthusiastic participant in the witch hunts. When she was cried out as a witch, he withdrew his support, and her "unobtrusive excellence awed back delusion's tide" (Larcom 62). In Longfellow's drama in iambic pentameter *Giles Corey of the Salem Farms* (1868), Corey is the tragic hero and Judge Hathorne the villain, while Cotton Mather speaks his own published words and is redeemed at the end. Mary E. Wilkins Freeman takes the same subject in her *Giles Corey, Yeoman* (1893). Neither playwright calls for depicting onstage Corey's last hours as he suffers "peine forte et dure," pressed to death under stones for standing mute and refusing to plead guilty or not guilty to the charge of witchcraft. In 1890, Charlotte Perkins Gilman collaborated with her friend Grace Ellery Channing on a revisionist view of the Salem witch belief, an unpublished and unproduced play *In the Name of the King! A Colonial Romance* (Lockwood, "Charlotte").

Most literary works in the twentieth century that deal with Salem are, if anything, anti-Gothic, attempting to rationalize what Cotton Mather called "praeternatural" happenings. The figure of Tituba, the Dark Other, is an exception. Although nothing in the trial transcripts refers to her teaching the circle of afflicted girls voodoo practices—let alone dancing with them in the woods, as in Miller's *The Crucible* (1953)—that legend began in the nineteenth century and can still be heard on tours of Salem. Longfellow's Tituba is portrayed as an exultant practicing witch who had studied "obi" in the West Indies. Ann Petry, the African American author of *Tituba of Salem Village*

(1964), a novel for young readers, does not join in the othering of Tituba and instead focuses on the lives and voices of the enslaved persons and indentured servants who become accusers. Marion Starkey and Shirley Jackson also produced well-researched accounts published as children's books that do not repeat the "voodoo priestess" legend. A postmodern take on that legend comes from the francophone Afro-Caribbean Maryse Condé, in whose novel of magical realism *I, Tituba, Black Witch of Salem* (1992), Tituba encounters Hawthorne's Hester Prynne in jail. Esther Forbes, known today for historical novels such as *Johnny Tremain* (1948), published the unabashedly Gothic *A Mirror for Witches* in 1928. Written in the voice of a Puritan divine, the novel delineates the damnation that awaited both witches and victims of witchcraft. Also incorporating the supernatural and reflecting feminist critique and recent scholarship on the witch hunts are Katherine Howe's *The Physick Book of Deliverance Dane* (2009) and Alice Hoffman's *Magic Lessons* (2020), the "prequel" to her best-selling *Practical Magic* (1995).

A few older short stories treat the witch belief as reality rather than a plot device. A rip-roaring yarn written and illustrated by Howard Pyle, "The Salem Wolf" (1909) adds werewolves to the witch's curse story, set "in the year when witches were so malignant at Salem" (1). Wilkins Freeman's "The Little Maid at the Door" (1898) is a ghost story set during the witch trials.

The most influential vision of the New England witch belief remains Arthur Miller's *The Crucible*, whose mapping of the Salem hysteria onto the Red Scare of his own time added the term "witch-hunting" to the American political lexicon. He declares in a "Note on Historical Accuracy" prefaced to every printing, "This play is not history in the sense in which the word is used by the academic historian." Nevertheless, the play continues to be taught as history in high schools and colleges. The actions of the Salem officials and the emphasis on naming names or refusing to do so make the allegory seem obvious to us now, but this did not prevent the play from achieving Broadway success in 1953. Three years before *The Crucible*, the poet William Carlos Williams also identified the Salem witch hunts with the McCarthy hearings in *Tituba's Children*, commissioned by an opera company, with libretto and lyrics by Williams.[12] This text makes explicit connections with the congressional investigation: the two times are brought together as the same actors play characters in 1692 and 1950. A Greek chorus reminds us: "Now it approaches, the / three-hundred-year-old curse / that has been the scourge of our country. [...] Intolerance and the whispering / of scandal" (1961: 292). The death

---

12. The company refused to perform *Tituba's Children*; it was not published until 1961, after the Broadway success of Miller's *The Crucible*. Williams's ambitious musical drama has never been professionally staged.

of Giles Corey is kept offstage, though linked to the McCarthy hearings. As the Voice is heard crying, "More weight! More weight!" the senator asks the protagonist: "Mr. McDee, have you ever been a member of the Communist Party?" and the hero replies, "I refuse to answer" (288).

A recent drama that takes the witch trials seriously and echoes many of Mather's own words as well as his title is *Wonders of the Invisible World* (2013) by playwright Liz Duffy Adams, who, as she states on her website, lives in "Western Mass on Pocumtuc and Nipmuc land" (*Liz*). This play, set in 1702, imagines a future for two of Salem's "afflicted girls," Abigail Williams and Mercy Lewis, who disappear from the historical record after the trials. Adams corrects one instance of Arthur Miller's admitted tampering with history; he had transformed Williams, 12 years old during the trials, into a temptress who has an affair with one of the condemned witches, John Proctor, Miller's common-man hero. Adams's play links the witch trials with fears of the Black Man in the forest and with the Indian attacks on the Maine frontier that had killed their families and caused Williams, Lewis, and other "afflicted girls" to take refuge in Salem, reminding us of Mary Beth Norton's theory that psychological trauma from these events caused their affliction.

During the Essex County panic in 1692, Gloucester was troubled not only by witches but also by the "Phantom Leaguers" chronicled in Cotton Mather's *Magnalia Christi*. These solid-appearing spirits tormented the prominent Babson family and brought the militia out to fight "strangers who appeared like Frenchmen" (Pringle 31). Local clergyman John Emerson wrote to Mather: "All rational persons will be satisfied [...] that the devil and his angels were the cause of all that befell the town" (qtd. in Pringle 32). Whittier retells the story in "The Garrison of Cape Ann" (1860). Unlike Mather, his soldiers fall to prayer and thus drive away the "ghostly leaguers," who in the original account vanished as inexplicably as they arrived. Whittier's headnote relegates the tale to "the childhood of its people," while granting it "the fitness and the freshness of an undecaying truth" (*Poems* 222).

A later encounter with spectral French and Indians occurred in 1754 in Windham, Connecticut, where the militia were called to arms on the town green to repel nocturnal invaders. They heard harrowing cries but never saw their attackers. In the morning, the bodies of numerous bullfrogs were found, supposedly victims of a drought that had forced them from their dried-up pond. The "Windham Frog-fight" made the town an object of ridicule and is commemorated in ballads, an opera, and huge bronze statues of golden-eyed frogs atop a local bridge (Ringel, *New* 80–81).

Gloucester's still-wild "Dogtown" is a nexus of Gothic legends, witchcraft, eccentric recluses, and murder, explored by Elyssa East in *Dogtown: Death and Enchantment in a New England Ghost Town* (2009). Long after the days of the witch trials, Dogtown was home to Old Peg Wesson, who in 1745 revenged herself upon soldiers who had insulted her by following them to the siege of Louisburg in the form of a crow. One soldier shot her with a silver button from his tunic; meanwhile back in Gloucester, the suspected witch died with a silver bullet in her wounds (Babson 321). In 1919, journalist Sarah Comstock found Salem too commercialized (nothing has changed in a century!), but upon reaching the notorious "Dogtown," she exclaimed, "'We are in the true home of the witches at last!'" (11). Brown University professor and scholar of the occult S. Foster Damon's pageant play *Witch of Dogtown* (1955) is based on these legends.

Puritans had earlier visitations from even stranger realms: the first sighting of an unidentified flying object (UFO) in the New World. Governor John Winthrop's *Journal* for 1639 reported: "a great light in the night at Muddy River [modern Brookline, Massachusetts]" (1: 294); no widespread panic ensued.

Puritan identification of Indian spirituality with Satan left "devil names" littering the New England landscape. Devil's Hopyard in East Haddam, Connecticut, its kettle holes explained as the place where the devil brewed his hops for witches, inspired stories by Hawthorne and Lovecraft. In reality it was sacred ground where pow-wows are still held. In Harriet Beecher Stowe's *Oldtown Fireside Story* "How to Fight the Devil," storyteller Sam Lawson explains the provenance of the nearby "Devil's Den":

"What do they call this his den for?"

"that 'are was in old witch times. There used to be witch meetins' held here, and awful doins'; they used to have witch sabba' days and witch sacraments, and sell their souls to the old boy." (193–94)

The young narrator's words in this tale echo my own experience and my attraction to the Gothic:

To me, the very idea of going to the Devil's Den was full of a pleasing horror. [...] I always lived in the shadowy edge of that line which divides spirit land from mortal life. [...] The old graveyard where, side by side, mouldered the remains of Indian sachems and the ancients of English blood, was my favorite haunt. (Stowe, *Oldtown Fireside* 191)

In "The Tartarus of Maids" (1855), Herman Melville likens a paper mill in western Massachusetts to an anteroom of Hell, entered through a gorge called

"The Devil's Dungeon." In "Ethan Brand," Hawthorne compares a flaming lime kiln in the same location to a "private entrance to the infernal regions" (103). Maine native and journalist Edward Page Mitchell, who published his folkloric Gothic stories as fact in the *New York Sun*, called "The Cave of the Splurgles" (1877) "the back door of hell." His Yankee narrator falls from Canaan, Vermont, into the realm of Ahriman and Beelzebub—and discovers that they are "as staid and respectable as the honest citizens who met nightly in Deacon Plympton's grocery."

Shrewd Yankees were rumored to have sought deals with the devil. The most famous, the real General Jonathan Moulton of New Hampshire, reputedly sold his soul for as much gold as would fill his boot. The devil poured gold down the chimney, but Moulton had removed the boot's sole; he lived a long, rich life before giving up his own. Called by Whittier the "Yankee Faust," he was the subject of *The Moulton Tragedy*, a lengthy "heroic poem" by S. Foster Damon (1970). Melville recalls this folklore of deals with the devil in "The Lightning-Rod Man" (1856). New England's version of the Flying Dutchman, Peter Rugg, "the missing man," is doomed to wander the roads as a harbinger of storms because he rashly vowed he would get home to Boston, despite of death or the devil. Created by journalist William Austin in 1824, Rugg's legend is incorporated into Hawthorne's satirical "A Virtuoso's Collection" (1854) and treated more sympathetically by Louise Imogen Guiney in her poem "Peter Rugg, the Bostonian" (1906). His story has passed into popular belief and can be found in folklore collections. Edward Page Mitchell printed as fact a similar story in "The Terrible Voyage of the Toad" (1878). This schooner's captain vows to sail her to the Paris Exposition, "'spite of blows or Beelzebub!" Another convincing bit of fakelore was created by Connecticut resident and Yale graduate Stephen Vincent Benét in "The Devil and Daniel Webster" (1936). In this story, which became a play, a folk opera, and a film, New Hampshire's legendary senator successfully defends a constituent, Jabez Stone, who has made the Faustian bargain. Benét's Old Scratch claims American citizenship: "When the first wrong was done to the first Indian, I was there. When the first slaver put out for the Congo, I stood on her deck" (24). Although this argument sounds progressive, Benét includes King Philip and Morton of Merry Mount on the jury of American traitors from Hell.

Not surprisingly, "new witch-land" abounds in tales of curses.[13] Connecticut's Micah Rood reputedly murdered a peddler in his orchard, who cursed the apple trees, which thereafter bore fruit with a red blood spot in the center. Though the peddler's curse may be legendary, the unique "Mike" apples were real, as was Micah Rood's family curse. His father, Thomas

---

13. See Citro, *Cursed in New England*.

Rood, was the only Puritan to be executed for incest, not originally a crime in Connecticut's legal code, when he fathered a son on his daughter, who was whipped but not hanged for that crime (P. H. Woodward). Midwesterner Elia Peattie retells the story as a female Gothic in "The Crime of Micah Rood" (1888). Nick Checker's short film "The Curse of Micah Rood" (2008) sides with Micah, whose cursed apple tree produced fruit well into the twentieth century. The contorted shape of these old fruit trees and their persistence around the ruins of human habitations are noted by Hawthorne in his preface to *Mosses from an Old Manse:*

> And what is more melancholy than the old apple trees that linger about the spot where once stood a homestead, but where there is now only a ruined chimney, rising out of a grassy and weed-grown cellar? They offer their fruit to every wayfarer—apples that are bittersweet with the moral of time's vicissitude. (1: 10)

Possession

> They made piteous Out cries, that they were cut with Knives. [...] Yea their Heads would be twisted almost round
> —*Magnalia Christi*, on the possession of the Goodwin children (1702)

Demonic possession with or without the intermediary of a human witch had been documented from the New Testament onward, and the Puritan divines were well-versed in that literature. In Connecticut, the possession of Ann Cole led to a witch hunt in Hartford and several hangings. Her case is documented as one of Increase Mather's *Remarkable Providences* (1684). Like many other energumens (humans possessed by demons), Cole spoke in foreign tongues—or at least in "Dutch-toned" English. Mather reports, "After the suspected witches were either executed or fled, Ann Cole was restored to health [...] approving herself a serious Christian" (*Remarkable* 99). There was an actual Dutch connection in this case: one woman accused and tried was Judith Varlet Bayard, sister-in-law of New York's governor Peter Stuyvesant, who rescued her and brought her to New York, a colony without judicial witch hunts.

Connecticut's witch trials—and there were many, extending from 1639 to 1702—have not been studied as extensively as the Salem panic; they are not as well-known to the American public. Recently, there has been some movement toward memorials and a pardon for the victims (not yet issued).[14] The accusations, trials, and executions in Connecticut seem to have inspired no Gothic fiction.

---

14. See documents of Connecticut's witch hunts in Hall; Taylor; Tomlinson; Burr.

One historical novel for young readers, Elizabeth George Speare's *The Witch of Blackbird Pond* (1958), a Newbery Prize winner, concerns a fictional witch trial in Wethersfield, along with real events surrounding Connecticut's hidden colonial charter. The minister Gershom Bulkeley appears as a character, but Speare says nothing about his successful argument against the use of "spectral evidence" that saved the accused witch Katherine Harrison in 1669. To the question of "Whether the preternatural apparitions of a person legally proved, be a demonstration of familiarity with ye devill?" Bulkeley responded that "it is not the pleasure of ye Most High, to suffer the wicked one to make an undistinguishable representation of any innocent person in a way of doing mischiefe, before a plurality of witnesses" (Taylor). Once accepted, this precedent made obtaining a conviction of witchcraft as a capital crime nearly impossible in Connecticut. English common law did not reject the legality of spectral evidence until 1700, which meant the end of witch trials in New England, but not of the witch belief.

A similar case of possession leading to a witch hunt was that of the Goodwin family of Boston in 1688. Blame fell on an Irish Catholic woman, Goody Glover, who probably spoke Gaelic better than English; she was convicted and executed that year. The disturbances continued, and Cotton Mather took the possessed Martha Goodwin into his household, recording in *Memorable Providences* his conversations with the demon inhabiting her. He calls it "a Story all made up of Wonders! I have related nothing but what I judge to be true. [...] I challenge all men to detect so much as one designed Falshood, yea, or so much as one important Mistake, from the Egg to the Apple of it" (Burr 123). In 1692, Cotton Mather repeated the same pattern with another possessed girl, Mercy Short, whose life was a mirror of the New England Gothic. She was an Indian captive, ran afoul of Sarah Good in Salem, became possessed by the devil, and was exorcized by Mather—all before her 18th birthday. Mercy confirmed Mather's conspiracy theories, reporting that Spectres told her of witch meetings in Salem including "French Canadiens and Indian Sagamores" (Burr 282).

In 1679, Increase Mather reported "the relation concerning the daemon" that tormented the Morse family of Newbury, Massachusetts, with what we now call poltergeist activity: Mather concludes, "The true reason of these strange disturbances is as yet not certainly known: some [...] did suspect Morse's wife to be guilty of witchcraft" (*Remarkable* 110). That suspicion led to a trial, but Elizabeth Morse was not convicted as a witch. A similar case at Great Island, New Hampshire, in 1682 is recounted in *Lithobolia* by an eyewitness, lawyer Richard Chamberlayne (1698). These attacks by what he called a "stone-throwing devil" were blamed on a neighbor's witchcraft: again, there were no convictions. The showers of stones, pounding noises, and moving furniture experienced during these events are staples of today's paranormal investigations. Shirley Jackson's Gothic classic *The Haunting of Hill House* (1959) illustrates these phenomena and more.

Demonic possession is a trope that lives today in life as much as in fiction. Strangely, New England's writers of Gothic horror have rarely dealt with the historical cases of poltergeist and possession. Norma Farber retells Mather's exorcism in *Mercy Short: A Winter Journal* (1982), designed for young readers. Harriet Prescott Spofford's "Her Story" (1872), set in its own time, reads like a narrative of possession. The narrator has been committed by her husband to a "Retreat" (private mental hospital) because he has been bewitched by another woman. Spofford's language echoes Poe's: the narrator denies madness; the other woman's hair is "hyacinthine" and falls in "great snake-like coils" (225). In language familiar to us from the seventeenth-century narratives of demonic possession, the narrator is tormented by bat-like spirits: "oh what loathsome-ness the obscene creatures whispered!" (231). Like the afflicted girls, she behaves badly in church under the eyes of her minister husband.

In the twentieth century, Ed and Lorraine Warren of Monroe, Connecticut, gained fame for investigating the Amityville Horror, the haunted house on Long Island supposedly built over the dwelling and grave of an accused Salem witch and an Indian burial ground—two master tropes of the New England Gothic. These modern-day demon hunters and exorcists were witnesses in Connecticut's "demon murder," the first in modern times in which the defense argued that the accused murderer was innocent by reason of demonic possession. The argument failed to sway the jury, and he was convicted. The Warrens' exploits have inspired films such as *The Haunting in Connecticut* (2009) and *The Conjuring* (2013), a successful franchise whose most recent installment *The Conjuring 3: The Devil Made Me Do It* (2021) retells their involvement in the 1981 case. In New England, everything old is new again.

Lifelong New Englander Paul Tremblay combines the trope of possession with reality TV in the Gothic novel *Head Full of Ghosts* (2015), an homage to Shirley Jackson's *We Have Always Lived in the Castle*. Jackson's and Tremblay's novels match Tzvetan Todorov's theory of the fantastic, defined as that literary moment in which neither the narrator(s) nor the readers of a work can be certain whether the events transpiring are supernatural, a dream, or symptoms of insanity. Tremblay says that this question of madness or demonic possession is his thesis (if novels are allowed to have a thesis): "What does that say about you or anyone else that my sister's nationally televised psychotic break and descent into schizophrenia wasn't horrific enough?" (112). In postmodern style, the surviving sister of the possessed girl writes a blog about the TV show that documented this possession; she invokes the Gothic tradition from *The Castle of Otranto* to "The Yellow Wall-paper" to describe her haunted house.

She asks, "Is the Barrett House telling us that our own diabolically challenged and/or mentally-ill Marjorie is the young woman trapped in the room with the wallpaper, or the metaphorical oppressed woman in the yellow wallpaper who yearns to be free?" (239). In the seventeenth century or the twenty-first, the drama of exorcism is enacted in the haunted house; the possessed subject continues to be female, the exorcist male, and the process of exorcism provides entertainment for the communal gaze.

Chapter 3

HAUNTING THE MASTER'S HOUSE

And said, as plain as whisper in the ear, The place is Haunted!
　　　　　—Thomas Hood, "The Haunted House" (1844)

In Providence, Rhode Island, in 1885, a woman bore a child and suffered from postpartum depression. Her artist husband suggested treatment with the "rest cure" championed by then-famous doctor and novelist S. Weir Mitchell: "Never to touch pen, brush or pencil again" and live a "normal" domestic life (Gilman, "Why" 348). Three months of following this prescription sent her from depression to "the border line of utter mental ruin" (349). The experience inspired her story "The Yellow Wall-paper" (1892); the writer Charlotte Perkins Gilman became famous as a feminist and author of nonfiction, poetry, and stories—some of which are Gothic—including a more traditional ghost story "The Giant Wistaria" (1891), whose Puritan adulteress recalls Hester Prynne. She and her dead baby haunt a site that has been doubly crushed by the patriarchy, immolated within a covered well in a house strangled by the titular wistaria vine.[1]

In the mid-1940s, a California-born woman moved with her professor husband to a small town in Vermont, where they were treated with suspicion by the residents. Later, she would claim that they pelted her with stones when she went on errands in the village. This experience was one inspiration for "The Lottery," Shirley Jackson's most famous story.

These brilliant short stories exemplify several strands of New England's Gothic fiction: psychological breakdown and immurement, the haunted house, and folk horror, with its survival of rituals performed in isolated backwaters though their significance has been lost. Among the most frequently anthologized and assigned in secondary schools and colleges, "The Yellow Wall-paper" and "The Lottery" feature female protagonists who are literally or

---

1. Gilman's short stories have been the subject of extensive critical analysis. See Gilbert and Gubar 89–92; Lockwood, *Archives* chap. 4; and Lockwood, "Charlotte," for feminist and queer readings, while Davison, "Haunted," places "The Yellow Wall-paper" in the context of the American female Gothic.

figuratively crushed by the patriarchal order. This chapter deploys the term "Domestic Gothic" for this tradition, emphasizing the contrast with the "Frontier Gothic" of Chapter 2. Rather than fearing attacks by wild beasts or savage men, the female protagonists of the Domestic Gothic fear those who share their homes—they fear being walled up in interior spaces with the walls closing in. Rather than celebrating or lamenting the loss of the native peoples or sublime landscapes, other female protagonists welcome or mourn for the apparitions of beloved mates and children. In verse and in prose, generations of women—and some men—have chronicled the horrors of the Domestic Gothic, while others shared or exposed Spiritualist mediums' hopes of a better afterlife.

The Domestic Gothic and Women's Ghost Stories

A narrow house with roof so darkly low
The heavy rafters shut the sunlight out;
One cannot stand erect without a blow;
Until the soul inside
Shrieks for a grave—more wide.
—Charlotte Perkins Gilman, "In Duty Bound" (1895)

The long nineteenth century was a golden age for women writing ghost stories, whether supernatural or explained. Jeffrey Andrew Weinstock's *Scare Tactics: Supernatural Fiction by American Women* (2008) argues that these writers replaced the terror of the unknown characteristic of the male Gothic tradition with the terror of the known, the difficulties of living as the Angel in the (haunted) House. Critics have proposed various nomenclature for the women's Gothic tradition. In "Getting Their Knickers in a Twist: Contesting the 'Female Gothic' in Charlotte Dacre's *Zofloya*," Carol Margaret Davison surveys "the major theoretical engagements with the 'Female Gothic,'" which is "an especially vexed, yet exciting and expanding, category within Gothic Studies."[2] The authors as well as the protagonists of this mode are mainly women. Domestic Gothic seems a more appropriate term for these women who live in ordinary homes, not castles or manor houses. While British female Gothic novels are often read as coming-of-age narratives for their young heroines, the protagonists of the New England Domestic Gothic are mainly older spinsters or widows. Gilbert and Gubar note that the Gothic is not the only genre in which women writers from Austen to

---

2. See also Wallace and Smith 1–12, 33.

the present have dealt with "the same concern with spatial constrictions" (83). Behind the veil of the supernatural, however, the authors of women's ghost stories could deal with such dangerous subjects as abusive husbands and abused children, resentment over women's limited options, madness, and same-sex desire, while still being accepted for publication in popular magazines.

These female writers of ghost stories were immensely popular in their own time, part of what Hawthorne called in an 1855 letter to his publisher, "a d—d mob of scribbling women" who were carrying all before them with the American public (*Letters* 177). The first generation of these writers, including Lydia Maria Child and Harriet Beecher Stowe, were active as reformers and feminists. Stowe inserted "An Authentic Ghost Story" into *Uncle Tom's Cabin*; the chapter title refers to the stratagem by which two of his female slaves gain freedom by haunting the godless and superstitious Simon Legree. Other New England women publishing supernatural fiction along with naturalistic "local color" stories include Rose Terry Cooke, Annie Trumbull Slosson, Madeline Yale Wynne, Josephine Dodge Daskam Bacon, Alice Brown, Harriet Prescott Spofford, Mary E. Wilkins Freeman, Sarah Orne Jewett, and Edith Wharton, who used the western Massachusetts setting of her summer home The Mount for several supernatural tales, though her psychological ghost stories were mainly set outside of New England.

Annie Trumbull Slosson was born in Stonington, Connecticut, of "distinguished Colonial stock." Her friend Harriet Prescott Spofford praised her "inspired imagination" and "spirituality" (*Little* 147).[3] Slosson's many ghost stories include the affecting Christmas story "A Speakin Ghost" (1890) and "A Dissatisfied Soul" (1904). Her most domestically Gothic story must be "Dumb Foxglove" (1898), in which the ghost of a crippled child who in life composed strange "receipts" from biblical sources haunts a neighbor's kitchen and seasons her plain Vermont cooking with the ghosts of coriander seed and spikenard.

Madeline Yale Wynne, who lived much of her life in Deerfield, Massachusetts, in a domestic partnership with metalworker and artist Annie Cabot Putnam, published several supernatural stories. The mystery of the title of "The Little Room" (1895) is never explained: the isolated home of two spinsters in the Vermont hills is haunted by a room that is sometimes a luxurious feminine retreat and sometimes a china closet, depending on whether men are present.[4]

---

3. Slosson's popular nonfiction includes a guide to the fad of china-collecting central to the Colonial revival of the late nineteenth century; see Lockwood, "Shopping" 68.

4. For Lacanian and gender-studies readings of the story, see Weinstock, *Scare Tactics* 59–69.

Mary E. Wilkins Freeman was a commercially successful writer of "local color" regionalism; she was rediscovered in the 1970s by feminist critics who mainly focused on her non-supernatural stories. More recent criticism acknowledges her contribution to the New England Gothic. Joanne Karpinski in "The Gothic Underpinnings of Realism in the Local Colorists' No Man's Land" links post–Civil War New England, with its many unmarried or widowed "superfluous women" to Frontier Gothic; she claims that in stories by writers including Wilkins Freeman the "gothic elements expose the threat to female autonomy posed by male desire and by the gender-role constraints of nineteenth century social order that translate such desire into power." Wilkins-Freeman's ghost stories are unabashedly supernatural in their use of revenants to portray child abuse in "The Wind in the Rose-bush" (1902) and madness in "The Hall Bedroom" (1903) (*Collected*).

Not surprisingly, the descent into madness is a common theme in the Domestic Gothic: as in Todorov's theory of the fantastic, the stories often provide no resolution as to whether the female protagonist is haunted, insane, or reacting to the intolerable conditions of real life under the patriarchy. While "The Yellow Wall-paper" is the most famous example, Harriet Prescott Spofford's "Her Story," which preceded it in 1872, can be read all three ways. Josephine Dodge Daskam Bacon's "The Gospel" (1913) seems like a response to "The Yellow Wall-paper"; its protagonist thrives under the "rest cure" that maddened Gilman and her unnamed narrator. Bacon's protagonist is haunted in her rest home by the feeble gray ghost of "a woman writer that the doctor sent us here for a long, long time" (249); in a conclusion more chilling to us than any specter, she accepts the ghost's warning, embraces "the gospel of Martha," and resolves to do housework rather than brainwork in the future.

New England ghosts can be surprisingly unhorrific, whether explained away or accepted as otherworldly visitations. As Hawthorne wrote in 1847, reviewing Whittier's *The Supernaturalism of New England*, "A New England ghost does not elevate us into a spiritual region; he hints at no mysteries beyond the grave. [...] He throws aside even his shroud, puts on the coat and breeches of the times, and takes up the flesh-and-blood business of life" (131). Or as the plain-spoken narrator of Slosson's "A Dissatisfied Soul" states of the restless spirit of the title, who was "dead and buried, and had been for three whole weeks": "It was amazing to us, [...] only we sort of got used to it after a spell, as you do to anything" (Lundie 286).

Sarah Orne Jewett's "The Foreigner" (1900) is set in Dunnet Landing, Maine, the imagined coastal village of *The Country of the Pointed Firs* (1896). Despite the Gothic opening on a dark and stormy night, its ghost could not be more reassuring: a mother come to bring her daughter home. The story concludes with this Spiritualist insight: "When folks is goin' 'tis all natural.

[…] You know plain enough there's somethin' beyond this world; the doors stand wide open. 'There's somethin' of us that must still live on; we've got to join both worlds together an' live in one but for the other'" (166–67). Echoing this insight in another story, one of "Miss Tempy's Watchers" says, "I wish folks could come back just once, and tell us how 'tis where they've gone" (295), a Maine Yankee's paraphrase of Hamlet's "undiscovered country / from whose bourn no traveler returns." Jewett's Yankee magical realism encompasses oracles, curses, witchcraft, and ghosts both benevolent and malevolent. Dunnet Landing and Deephaven are imaginary spaces that reflect the real decay of Maine's maritime trade; their fishermen remember when fortunes could be made trading with the Spice Islands, and each generation has declined from the one before. As with Wilkins Freeman, Jewett's point-of-view characters are generally widows or spinsters; her narrators, women "from away." Almira Todd, White witch and herbalist of *The Country of the Pointed Firs*, was once courted by Captain Littlepage, who tells sea stories of adventure in the Far North, where he hears about "a kind of waiting-place between this world an' the next" (*Country* 39). According to Holly Jackson, "The New England Jewett portrays is just such a place, a strange northern country with 'fog-shaped' people (37) suspended between life and death" (284). W. S. Winslow's *The Northern Reach* (2021) revisits this bleak territory in a novel reminiscent of Jewett's technique of linked short stories.

Some nineteenth-century women writers (including Jewett) lived in long-term relationships with other women, dubbed by Henry James "Boston Marriages," and their ghost stories can be read as explorations of queer desire through a process Terry Castle terms the "Apparitional Lesbian." In thus characterizing Daniel Defoe's *The Apparition of Mrs. Veal* (1706) arguably the first nonbeliever's ghost story in English literary tradition, Castle defines the archetypal apparitional Lesbian plot: "The kiss that doesn't happen, the kiss that can't happen, because one of the women involved has become a ghost […] a kind of love that […] cannot be perceived, except apparitionally" (30). As Paulina Palmer writes in *Lesbian Gothic: Transgressive Fictions*, "Spectrality is especially well suited to articulating ideas of lesbian invisibility and the capacity of lesbian desire to survive oppression and 'return' in the manner of the Freudian concept of the repressed" (4). Harriet Prescott Spofford pays tribute to this circle of New England regionalists and writers of the supernatural in *A Little Book of Friends* (1916): Here, she describes the "Boston marriage" of her friends Annie Fields and Sarah Orne Jewett. "Before his death, Mr. Fields suggested Sarah Orne Jewett as a possible friend and companion for his wife in the future; and she gave Mrs. Fields great happiness" (18). "There and Here" (1897) by another member of this circle, New Hampshire native Alice Brown, is an uplifting, beautifully written supernatural story whose apparitional Lesbian subtext may be an allegory for her relationship with the poet Louise Imogen Guiney.[5] By an almost Gothic coincidence, Guiney was a childhood friend of Susan Phillips Lovecraft, mother of H. P. Lovecraft. In 1892–93, Guiney rented rooms in her house in Auburndale (now Newton), Massachusetts, to the family of the 2-year-old future writer of weird fiction.

Rose Terry Cooke's "My Visitation" (1858)[6] is a Bronte-esque Gothic novel in miniature, dealing explicitly with same-sex desire. The narrator proclaims her madness, then tells of her harrowing "visitation" by "It." Gradually, the vision becomes less horrific and resolves into the ghost of her beloved Eleanor, who "betrayed" her by marrying a man. The narrator learns to love a man as well but never with the passion of her first love that cannot be consummated except beyond the veil.

New England's nineteenth-century women writers were not limited to the Domestic Gothic or the genteel magazines. Some published in the penny press, stories that David Reynolds in *Beneath the American Renaissance* called sensation novels of dark adventure that recycled tropes from the first Gothic revival. Louisa May Alcott, the iconic children's author and daughter of transcendentalist Bronson Alcott, published sensation stories under pseudonyms during the 1860s. These thrillers were unearthed by Madeleine Stern and Leona Rostenberg, and published in a series beginning with the aptly titled *Behind a Mask* (1975). Gothic sensation could also be found in the annals of true crime. In 1892, Lizzie Borden, New England's most notorious spinster, was accused but never convicted of the axe murder of her father and stepmother. Britain's premier Gothicist Angela Carter spent a year at Brown University and became fascinated with the nearby occurrence. Her version of the story is "The Fall River Axe Murders" (1981); the house has become a Gothic tourist attraction, the Lizzie Borden B&B.

In the mid-twentieth century, Shirley Jackson combined the Domestic Gothic traditions of local color ghost stories with the Southern Gothic of ancestral secrets, class warfare, and decaying family mansions. Jackson created a new style of Domestic Gothic in the lightly fictionalized humorous sketches of life with her demanding husband and four children that she published in popular women's magazines and reshaped into collections whose titles ought to have warned readers of their subversive intent: *Life among the Savages* (1953) and *Raising Demons* (1957). She portrayed the witchcraft persecution, shunning, and resistance to change in modern suburban Gothic settings. Jackson, who lived for many years and died in North Bennington, Vermont, was a best-selling author in the mid-twentieth century who has only recently

---

5. See Weinstock, *Scare Tactics* 154–62; Salmonson 135–36.
6. See Weinstock, *Scare Tactics* 142–54.

been recognized as central to the American Gothic. Her works encompass the grotesque *We Have Always Lived in the Castle* as well as the classic ghost story *The Haunting of Hill House*, which never rationalizes the malignancy of its supernatural threat. She specifies no state for its setting, yet it is clearly somewhere in New England, with its unhospitable attitude to visitors and towns named East Barrington and Ashton. With its angles and measurements that are all "slightly wrong" (105), Hill House haunts the psychic researchers who attempt to study it as well as those who dare to read about it. Whether writing about haunted houses or haunted minds, Jackson's subject is always the evil that lies just beneath the surface of everyday life. Her life's work is honored by the yearly Shirley Jackson Awards "for outstanding achievement in the literature of psychological suspense, horror, and the dark fantastic" that are voted on by "a jury of professional writers, editors, critics, and academics" ("The Shirley").

Jackson's second novel—the psychological Gothic *Hangsaman* (1951)—was partly inspired by the disappearance of Bennington College undergraduate Paula Welden. This unsolved mystery is one of many such unexplained absences around Glastenbury Mountain, dubbed by Citro the "Bennington Triangle." In addition to legends about monsters and mountain men, at least five well-documented cases of disappearances occurred between 1945 and 1951, and only one body was recovered (*Passing* 87–95). The first feature film of low-budget horror producer Del Tenney, *Psychomania* (1963), was inspired by his wife's memories of her Bennington classmate's disappearance (Bissette, "The Gods"). In Donna Tartt's novel *The Secret History* (1992), several classics students at a lightly disguised Bennington College get up to no good in the woods, kill a farmer, and sacrifice one of their own, whose death is treated as another unexplainable disappearance. Tartt's novel is called "Schoolhouse Gothic" by Sherry R. Truffin, a tradition she identifies with examples ranging from Poe's "William Wilson" through Maine writer Elizabeth Hand's *Waking the Moon* to Harry Potter's haunted Hogwarts. "In the Schoolhouse Gothic, school is experienced as psychological and social trauma, and it transforms students into sociopaths, machines, or zombies" (Truffin 165). Stephen King's *Carrie* (1974), whose psychically powerful protagonist is traumatized by her classmates and takes horrifying revenge, could be considered another example of Schoolhouse Gothic.

Dangerous survivals of Old World cults feature in Thomas Tryon's *Harvest Home* (1973), a novel of folk horror published during a film boom in this genre best known through Britain's *The Wicker Man*. Set in Connecticut, the cult film *Let's Scare Jessica to Death* (1971) features a vampire (not the New England type discussed in Chapter 4) who preys upon city folks who buy a backwoods farmhouse. Though the term "folk horror" was not in use at the time, Steve Bissette notes that something must have been going on in Vermont's dark hills, "tied [...]

with the land itself: an alchemy of rocks, soil, and celluloid," together with the influx of outsiders forming communes on that land. Vermont indie films made from the point of view of those hippies and cultists include "Transformation" (1972), a vignette of a Wiccan coven filmed by a feminist collective; director Walter Ungerer's *Solstice*; and his first feature-length film *The Animal* (1976). Another Vermont film, *Dark August* (1976), follows the familiar pattern of the "flatlander" coming to grief in the mountains. He runs down the daughter of a wizard and is cursed by him, haunted by robed figures in the woods, and aided by a "good witch" psychic (Bissette, "The Gods").

New England's Gothic Verse

All are vanish'd, all have fled,

Save the memories of the dead.

—Lydia Huntley Sigourney, "Removal of an
Ancient Mansion" (1854)

Male and female Gothic traditions may be found in New England's poetry. The region's greatest poet of the Gothic must be Emily Dickinson, whose preoccupation with death and horror led cultural provocateur Camille Paglia to dub her "Amherst's Madame de Sade" in *Sexual Personae* (1990). Daneen Wardrop goes further in cataloguing *Emily Dickinson's Gothic* (1996), including her themes of immurement, haunting, the apocalyptic, and the transports of fear. Dickinson wrote to T. W. Higginson: "Nature is a Haunted House—but Art—a House that tries to be haunted" (qtd. in Paglia 659). Once they are read as Gothic, poems such as "'Twas like a Maelstrom with a Notch" with its hellish vision of "a Goblin with a Gauge" become spectral evidence for Dickinson's haunted art. Gilbert and Gubar make Dickinson their emblem of "the loneliness of the female artist" and "the woman writer's struggle for artistic self-definition" (50); in the mode of the Domestic Gothic, however, it seems that women writers could find a safe space and, for some, community and commercial success.

Lydia Sigourney was famous (and satirized) for writing poetic elegies for dead friends and dead infants, though her unfailing faith kept her tributes to cemeteries and their occupants from taking a more Gothic turn. Known as "the Sweet Singer of Hartford," she was born and grew up in Norwich, Connecticut. She wrote poems on Connecticut ghost legends such as "The Bell of the Wreck" (Sigourney, *The Western* 212–14), based on the belief that the bell of the steamer *Atlantic*, wrecked in Long Island Sound, could be heard tolling for the dead long afterward. Louise Imogen Guiney, companion of Alice Brown, wrote a few poems based on New England legends but was primarily interested in the "real Middle Ages" of Chaucer, chivalry and saints' lives.

Other poets transformed New England legends into Gothic verse. Whittier's most Gothic poem may be his most famous: *Snow-Bound* (1865). Around the hearth, the family hear reminiscences of colonial days, tales of witches and Indian raids. The poet's mother spins and knits and tells "how the Indian hordes came down / [...] And how her own great-uncle bore / His cruel scalp-mark to fourscore" (24). The same picture of a storyteller conjuring visions of the New England past is Sam Lawson of Stowe's *Oldtown Fireside Tales* (1872): he tells ghost stories to delight and harrow his audience, when "Two-thirds of New England was then dark, unbroken forests, through whose tangled paths the mysterious winter wind groaned and shrieked and howled with weird noises" (3).

Whittier's *Snow-Bound* does not simply retell legends: it can be read as an invocation of natural magic, with its epigraph from the wizard Agrippa. In "The Supernaturalism of Snow-Bound," Lewis H. Miller argues that the poem's title can be understood at multiple levels: the extended family is held captive by the snow, removed from the outside world, but read "within a context of supernaturalism: 'snow-bound' describes an imaginative attempt at 'binding' a tempest so that the storm [...] 'shall do no hurt'" (307). Miller adds that "snow-bound" could refer to the book itself, with Whittier the wizard of words who can bind the past within its covers. These lines near the end of the poem support Miller's reading and provide an emblem for the allure of the Gothic: "Clasp, Angel of the backward look [...] / The brazen covers of thy book; The weird palimpsest old and vast, / Wherein thou hid'st the spectral past" (*Snow-Bound* 50). The spectral associations of Whittier's poem inspired David Goudsward to commission stories from contemporary writers of Gothic horror for *Snowbound with Zombies: Tales of the Supernatural Inspired by the Life & Work of John Greenleaf Whittier*, a benefit for the Whittier homestead in Haverhill, Massachusetts, where the poem was set.

Whittier's fellow "Household Poet" Longfellow was also one of America's first scholarly medievalists. His ambitious project to retell Chaucer's *Canterbury Tales* as *Tales of a Wayside Inn* (1863) mingles local history ("Paul Revere's Ride") with translations from the Norse sagas and Boccaccio. The setting is a colonial inn in Sudbury, Massachusetts, which was abandoned in Longfellow's time. The "Prelude"—similar to Chaucer's General Prologue—limns the Gothic setting:

A kind of old Hobgoblin Hall,
Now somewhat fallen to decay,

With weather-stains upon the wall,
And stairways worn, and crazy doors,
And creaking and uneven floors.
(Longfellow, *Tales* 1–2)

Restored by Henry Ford and reopened as Longfellow's Wayside Inn, today its haunted reputation attracts ghost hunters.

Robert Frost's sinister hill wives, witches, and dead hired men fit comfortably into the British Gothic tradition of narrative poems. His early supernatural poems include "The Witch of Coos" and "The Pauper Witch of Grafton" (1923) and "Ghost House" (1915). The speaker in the latter haunts a cellar hole marking an abandoned farmhouse:

I dwell in a lonely house I know
That vanished many a summer ago,
And left no trace but the cellar walls,
And a cellar in which the daylight falls.
(Frost, *Boy's* 12)

"Home Burial" and "The Fear" (1914) are Gothic vignettes that seem like stories partially told, ghosts whose histories remain unsaid (Frost, *North*).

Like Hawthorne, Robert Lowell (of the Boston Lowells who speak only to the Cabots who speak only to God) was haunted by his witch-hunting, Indian-killing Puritan ancestors. His Pulitzer Prize–winning collection *Lord Weary's Castle* (1946), whose title comes from a medieval ballad, includes poems meditating on the legacy of King Philip's War in "At the Indian Killer's Grave" (54–57); on the persecution of Quakers, whale hunting, and *Moby-Dick* in "The Quaker Graveyard in Nantucket" (8–12); and on the ill fate of spiders and Puritan souls in "Mr. Edwards and the Spider" (58–59).

Spiritualism Opens the Gates

The spirit-world around this world of sense
Floats like an atmosphere, and everywhere
Wafts through these earthly mists and vapors dense
A vital breath of more ethereal air
—Henry Wadsworth Longfellow, "Haunted Houses" (1858)

The advent of Spiritualism gave nineteenth-century New Englanders a more positive vision of the Other World than that prescribed by Puritan doctrine. Ann Braude's *Radical Spirits: Spiritualism and Women's Rights in Nineteenth-Century*

America analyzes the appeal of this woman-centered theology that created a religion based on communicating with the dead through a human medium. In 1848, four years after the first telegraph messages were sent in Morse code, the Fox sisters in upstate New York began delivering messages from the world of spirits through a code of raps. Harriet Beecher Stowe was a Spiritualist adherent as were many of the first women's rights advocates. The table in Seneca Falls, New York, upon which the Declaration of Women's Rights was signed resounded with spirit rapping. Spiritualism occasioned a new type of Gothic literature, with specters who were welcome rather than appalling; Heaven itself looked like New England in Elizabeth Stuart Phelps's best seller *The Gates Ajar* (1868) and its sequels. Phelps's apparitional Lesbian story "Since I Died" (1873) is narrated by the ghost herself, but unlike the stories discussed earlier, it is clear that their relationship in life was a passionate one. There is no sense of fear in this Spiritualist afterlife, but the ghostly narrator cannot reveal Death's secrets to her lover. Another New Englander, Elizabeth Oakes Smith, was a prominent Spiritualist preacher, poet, and collector of ghost legends. She defines the New England Gothic in her autobiographical *Shadow Land, or, The Seer* (1852) as based upon "the experience of the first settlers [...] surrounded by wild beasts, by merciless and treacherous savages, and the gloom of immeasurable forests—weighed by solitude, isolation, and religious asperity" (121). She claims that the families descended from those settlers whom she encountered in southern Maine retained faculties of precognition and ghost seeing.

The new Spiritualist religion was not universally approved, nor did everyone endorse these attempts to make the dead speak. Nineteenth-century texts refer to the phenomena as "the modern necromancy" (Sargent, "Planchette" 169) and link spiritualism to witchcraft. Conservative Protestants condemned the mediums and the followers of Spiritualism as devil worshippers. In the polemic *Spiritualism and Necromancy* (1873), A. B. Morrison argues "that necromancy has only changed in name; that its practices are common to-day, in Europe and America, under the Christian name of spiritualism" (25). The accusation of "necromancer" has been leveled at Faust, Count Dracula, and Victor Frankenstein, but it is even more appropriately aimed at the Spiritualist mediums and at today's "Ghost Whisperers" who want to help the dead "cross over." The séance stands for necromancy normalized, old fears of power-hungry sorcerers calmed by the generally lower-middle-class and female medium. Since the nineteenth century, the utterances of the spirits they evoke have reassured the hearers that life beyond the veil can be as uninteresting and respectable as life on the earthly side.

Hawthorne's *The Blithedale Romance* was composed a few years into what he calls the "epoch of rapping spirits" (183). His figure of the Veiled Lady reminds us of the exploitation of female spirit mediums by ruthless showmen. Hawthorne comments on attempts to communicate with the dead, asking, "If these phenomena have not humbug at the bottom" and answering his question with, "These goblins, if they exist at all, are but the shadows of past mortality [...] adjudged unworthy of the eternal world" (183); he urges readers not to seek their company.

William Dean Howells, icon of American realism in the novel and drama, deals with the Spiritualist movement in *The Undiscovered Country* (1880). Though his science-minded protagonists debunk the phenomena of the séance, much of the novel treats the religion of Spiritualism respectfully. The two young men who disrupt a public test séance note that the presenter, the self-styled Doctor Boynton, comes from Maine, "the land of Norembega, the mystical city. The witches settled Maine, when they were driven out of Salem" (108), thus demonstrating Howells's knowledge of New England's Gothic history. As in *The Blithedale Romance*, Boynton tries and fails to combine mesmerism with his daughter's psychic mediumship. Still, Boynton is not as amoral as the impresario Westervelt in *The Blithedale Romance*, nor is he a leering Gothic villain like the hypnotist Svengali in George DuMaurier's *Trilby* (1894). Howells presents a relatively sympathetic portrait of the utopian communism of a Shaker village that shelters the indigent Spiritualists but refuses to adopt Boynton's ideas.

Howells's friend and literary rival Henry James is more dismissive of Spiritualism in *The Bostonians* (1886). He notes the subversive and empowering effects of the movement while caricaturing these feminists as deluded witches.

It was one of those weird meetings she was so fond of.

"What kind of meetings do you refer to? You speak as if it were a rendezvous of witches on the Brocken."

"Well, so it is; they are all witches and wizards, mediums, and spirit-rappers, and roaring radicals." (1.6)

Sarah Helen Whitman of Providence was an ardent Spiritualist; she and her circle channeled Poe and published posthumous collaborations dictated by the deceased poet through automatic writing (Richards). Whitman had composed and sent a passionate valentine to the still-living Poe, which she later published as "The Raven" (Whitman, *Hours* 66). The poem imagines the poets visiting and commenting upon each other's created worlds, a spiritual telegraph that continued after Poe's death. Whitman dedicated the rest of her life to protecting his reputation, writing *Edgar Poe and His Critics* (1860) in response to Rufus Griswold's unflattering biography.

While women were prominent as trance mediums and Spiritualist lecturers, the most famous "physical medium" of the era was Daniel Dunglas Hume, born in Scotland but brought up in Connecticut. His feats were witnessed by Mark Twain, who later hosted séances at his home in Hartford. Internationally famous, Home was investigated by Britain's Society for Psychical Research and caricatured by Robert Browning as "Mr. Sludge, the Medium." This Yankee wizard even spent time at the court of the czar of Russia. Other well-known mediums were Vermont's Eddy Brothers, who attracted crowds to their circles and spirit cabinet in Chittenden. Henry Steel Olcott, a Civil War veteran, was sent to investigate them and concluded that the manifestations were authentic in his report *People from the Other World* (1875).[7] Current Vermonter Daniel Mills's *Moriah* focuses on the psychological trauma of the mediums and the investigator in a novel that hews closely to the facts. Indians and wounded soldiers appear as figures in the Spiritualist drama, as the repressed return in spectral form to bring messages to the survivors.

Poets continued to be fascinated by Spiritualism into the mid-twentieth century. Helen Sword in *Ghostwriting Modernism* details the use of automatic writing and Ouija boards by New England poets James Merrill and Sylvia Plath. Merrill based his masterpiece *The Changing Light at Sandover* (1982) on over twenty-five years of spirit communication sessions with his partner David Jackson at his home in Stonington, Connecticut (Buckley and Merrill 415). The poet's answer to whether spirits had genuinely dictated the epic is "I don't care whether you believe the revelations as long as you believe that we had the experience" (420). Better known for her Gothic metaphors and allusions to the Tarot in her poetry, Plath recorded spirit communication sessions in the mid-1950s with her husband, Ted Hughes, in a poem "Dialogue over a Ouija Board" that Hughes relegated to a footnote in the volume of *Collected Verse* he edited after her death; Sword theorizes that it revealed too much about their marriage (138).

Spiritualism continues to exist as a religion, and psychics and mediums continue to attract customers. Old-style séances are less commonly found in recent New England fiction; an exception is Charles L. Grant's "A Night of Dark Intent," in which the séance participants in the old Tudor mansion of his imagined Connecticut town of Oxrun Station turn out to be "not quite dead" themselves (73). The principles of spiritualism are more frequently demonstrated in the form of "scientific" ghost hunting, as evidenced by the number of "Reality" TV shows featuring paranormal investigators. One of the earliest and most successful of these organizations is The Atlantic Paranormal Society (TAPS), based in Rhode Island.

---

7. For more on the Eddy Brothers and Olcott's investigation, see Citro, *Passing* 49–59.

Although the smallest state escaped the Puritan legacy of witch persecution, it became a nexus for the New England vampire belief. Rhode Island is even better known by the rest of the world as the home of H. P. Lovecraft, whose essays, letters, and fiction reflect the history and anxieties of the New England Gothic, and whose lantern jaw and deep-set eyes have become the literal "face" of the genre.

Chapter 4

BEYOND LOVECRAFT COUNTRY: RACISM, XENOPHOBIA, NEW DIRECTIONS

"What has cast such a shadow upon you?"
"The negro."
—Herman Melville, *Benito Cereno* (1856)

Enslaved Africans are skeletons in New England's closets. Frances Manwaring Caulkins's *History of Norwich* (1845) tells of "a poor negro slave, named Jock," who "hung himself in prison" in the eighteenth century because he had "in a fit of jealousy and anger" shot his lady friend. "His body was given to the elder Dr. Turner for dissection, and his bones formed into an anatomical figure, [...] an object of terror and curiosity to the ignorant and the children of the neighborhood" (341). After Dr. Turner's death, pranksters would abstract the skeleton on Halloween until the bones disappeared, with no notion of a proper burial. I have retold the story of "Old Jock's Bones" on many a Gothic tour. Another enslaved man from Waterbury, Connecticut, who continued to serve after death, was immortalized by Marilyn Nelson in *Fortune's Bones: The Manumission Requiem.*

Fortune was a slave of bonesetter Dr. Preserved Porter, upon his death in 1798, his master boiled and labeled his bones. In Gothic fashion, descendants walled up the skeleton in their attic, where it was found and given to the Mattatuck Museum, all history lost. In 1996, the Museum assembled experts to learn more of this skeleton, which had been dubbed "Larry," and unearthed the tale of one of Waterbury's last enslaved people. One resident told Nelson, "I don't think anybody ever envisioned that this was truly a human being." (22)

A few miles away, in Litchfield County, James Mars was "Born and Sold in Connecticut," as he titled his autobiography (1869). He was inspired to write because in his old age he experienced the same inability of White residents to envision that "the land of good morals and steady habits, was [...] a slave state, and that slaves were driven through the streets tied or fastened together for market. [...] Yes, this was done in Connecticut" (37).

These skeletons and Mars's now-forgotten autobiography represent the erasure of New England's Gothic history of slavery and racial injustice as well as the restless persistence of dead bodies of color in Gothic fiction. In this chapter, we will find some Euro-American writers who have dealt with these ghosts directly, but more frequently writers of the Gothic and New England residents alike have projected their fears of loss of position, decline, and devolution onto other scapegoats—vampires, immigrants, the poor. Lovecraft created Gothic science fiction by transforming non-Nordic immigrants into aliens from other planets and dimensions who are worshipped as gods by the "inferior races" and invoked by inbred or ignoble specimens of the Anglo-Saxon race. Only recently have artists of color such as Connecticut poet Laureate Marilyn Nelson and filmmaker Jordan Peele, as well as White writers, directors, and critics, opened those skeleton-filled closets and by so doing questioned the validity of Lovecraft's vision of the New England Gothic.

Blackness and Power

> There was quite a number of negroes held here as slaves, nearly three hundred in number [...] shortly after the Revolution the negroes disappeared.
>
> —Pringle, *History of Gloucester* (1892)

This section's title plays on Harry Levin's *The Power of Blackness* (1958), a study of Melville, Hawthorne, and Poe, which argues—as did Leslie Fiedler in *Love and Death in the American Novel*—for the centrality of the Gothic mode in American literature. Fiedler identifies two sources of guilt simultaneously denied and expressed: the treatment of the native peoples and the chattel slavery and subsequent oppression of African Americans. Fiedler states that the "symbolic gothicism" of Hawthorne, Melville, Twain, and Faulkner "has never ceased to confront the problem of the Negro" (474). Writing three decades later, from the position of a Black woman and a novelist, Toni Morrison supports and questions this assertion. In *Playing in the Dark*, she argues that "the major and championed characteristics of our national literature—individualism, masculinity [...] the thematics of innocence coupled with an obsession with figurations of death and hell" are "responses to a dark, abiding, signing Africanist presence" (5). She notes that the literary response of the canonical authors was as often an absence as a confrontation. "Through significant

and underscored omissions, startling contradictions, heavily nuanced conflicts
[…] a real or fabricated Africanist presence was crucial to their sense of
Americanness" (6).

That "Africanist presence" in New England Gothic may be viewed like a
paper-cut silhouette by its absence or by its opposite, a preoccupation with
Whiteness. Melville and Poe entered that heart of darkness to be found within
the whiteness of the whale in *Moby-Dick* and in the Antarctic of Poe's *The
Narrative of Arthur Gordon Pym of Nantucket* (1838). Both works are based on
true stories of New Englanders' colonization of the world by sea. Melville's
Benito Cereno (1856) is another Gothic narrative of maritime New England,
based on the "Voyages and Travels" of Captain Amasa Delano of Duxbury,
Massachusetts. It may also have been inspired by the 1839 mutiny on the slave-
ship *Amistad*, which was taken by the Revenue Cutter Service and brought
to New London, Connecticut. Those enslaved mutineers were imprisoned,
tried, defended by former president John Quincy Adams before the Supreme
Court, and eventually freed. While Melville hews closely—sometimes word
for word—to Delano's original narrative, the Gothic elements of *Benito Cereno*
are Melville's alone: the skeleton figurehead, the hatchet sharpeners, and his
portrayal of the Negroes as pirates, demons, and animals. Aboard the haunted
ship, amid scenes of blood, perhaps the most chilling moment is Melville's
summary of Delano's mindset that enabled him to be convinced that the ship
was in the hands of its White masters instead of the mutineer slaves: "Captain
Delano took to negroes, not philanthropically, but genially, just as other men
to Newfoundland dogs" (201). Allan Lloyd-Smith links the work with anxieties
over slavery: "at the denouement, when Delano himself has his foot on the
neck of the unmasked Babo, Melville's story implies the hypocritical collusion
of the North with the peculiar institution of the South at the time of rising
pre–Civil War tension" (2012: 173). John C. Calhoun is credited with coining
the euphemism of "our peculiar institution," meaning special, unique to us,
for slavery in the South, yet as we have seen, slavery continued far too long in
the North. Today, the image of Delano's foot on Babo's neck inevitably recalls
the 2020 murder of George Floyd.

Toni Morrison notes in *Playing in the Dark* "the strong affinity between the
nineteenth-century American psyche and gothic romance" and concludes
that the country needed to purge its guilt through this form (36). Morrison's
Beloved (1987) has come to define the more recent American Gothic response
to slavery, in the form of "cultural haunting." Kathleen Brogan argues that
Morrison's novel

> brings to the foreground the communal nature of its ghosts. When
> the ghost in Morrison's *Beloved* speaks of her life in the grave in terms

appropriate to the slave ships, she clearly becomes more than an externalization of one character's longing and guilt; her return represents the return of all dead enslaved Africans. Stories of cultural haunting differ from other twentieth-century ghost stories in exploring the hidden passageways not only of the individual psyche, but also of a people's historical consciousness. ("American")

Such hauntings body forth a society's complicity in evil and cannot be explained away by a single protagonist's insanity.

Ghosts are paradoxical: absent, yet present. Powerless shades, yet devastatingly powerful in their effect upon the living. In fiction, the haunting legacy of slavery and racial violence can seem an absence rather than a presence. It is central to the American South in the popular imagination, while New England's image is that of activism against slavery and for racial justice. Yet slavery flourished in New England for 150 years, even during the years following the abolition of the slave trade. The lines quoted in this section's epigraph come from the town history of Gloucester, Massachusetts; similar formulations can be found in other local histories. What *did* happen to New England's former slaves? Why does Catherine Sedgwick, in whose home in Stockbridge the petition to end slavery in Massachusetts had its origin, deny (in her 1853 article "Slavery in New England") that there were ever many slaves in that state? Sedgwick was a moderate abolitionist, who feared— rightly—that too radical a stance would lead to war. This may be why she failed to finish an antislavery novel that would have predated *Uncle Tom's Cabin* (Weierman).

The disappearance or erasure of New England's Black residents is traced by James Loewen in *Sundown Towns: A Hidden Dimension of American Racism* (2005). Loewen charts the decline in the African American population in the North, which he calls "The Great Retreat." For example, Maine before 1890 had at least a few Black residents in every county; by 1930 most of Maine's counties had none (55). Loewen attributes the decline to deliberate policies that prevented Blacks from residing in towns and suburbs, so-called sundown or sunset towns that prohibited Blacks from living there except as servants; restrictive real-estate covenants; and the 1920s revival of hate groups such as the Ku Klux Klan, which was active in the New England states, attacking Catholics and Jews as well as the diminished number of Black residents.

The definitive history of slavery in New England has yet to be written. Harriet Beecher Stowe composed *Uncle Tom's Cabin* (1852) while living in Brunswick, Maine, yet she never wrote about slavery in that state. Stowe shares a birthplace with the man who became Osawatomie John Brown. Both were born in Litchfield, Connecticut, while there were still enslaved men and women in the town, yet not until Stowe left New England did she become an abolitionist. She never wrote about the slave history of her native state. She might be dealing with this absence in "The Ghost in the Cap'n Brown House" from *Oldtown Fireside Tales*. In this example of "ghosting" slavery, even critics who read the story as feminist Gothic seem not to notice the presence of a living woman confined to the house: Quassia. Her status is not clearly defined, but Stowe's language is that of slavery: The Captain "had an old black Guinea nigger-woman [...] she used to wear a gret red turban and a yaller short gown and red petticoat, and a gret string o' gold beads round her neck, and gret big gold hoops in her ears, made right in the middle o' Africa among the heathen there" (142–43). The story's narrator loses interest in the Black servant to focus on the apparition of a White woman who may or may not have been alive. Quassia is another Negro who disappears.

The bewitching and ruthless narrator of Harriet Prescott Spofford's "The Amber Gods" (1863) casually notes "my great-grandfather was a sea-captain, and actually did bring home cargoes of slaves" (12), but she projects the evils of slavery and demons of colonialism upon an "Asian imp" (rather than an enslaved African). When carried to New England, the little imp destroys the master's house: "cut the noses out of the old portraits, and chewed the jewels out of the settings, killed the little home animals" (12).

Epes Sargent, a Bostonian who worked in New York, combines spiritualism with abolitionism and feminism in the novel *Peculiar: A Tale of the Great Transition*, published during the Civil War. The hero of the title is a fugitive slave "christened PECULIAR INSTITUTION" by a drunken overseer but known as Peek (22). Peek stows away on a schooner bound to New London, where a sympathetic abolitionist keeps him from being arrested like the *Amistad* mutineers. Involvement with Spiritualism transforms Peek's consciousness and eventually that of the slave-owning villain Col. Hyde:

Hyde saw heavy physical objects moved about, floated in the air, [...] without the intervention of any agencies recognized as material.

The hard, cold atheism of the man's heart was smitten, rent, and displaced. For the first time, he was made to feel that the body's death is but a process of transition in the soul's life. (467)

Sargent believes in the reality of the paranormal phenomena of levitation and clairvoyance, linking them to Cotton Mather's account of the exorcism of Margaret Rule and to his own experience of being touched by a spirit hand at a séance (37n).

Like Stowe, Sargent does not engage with the issue of slavery or racial vio-lence in the North, nor did *Peculiar* inspire imitators of its mixture of Gothic melodrama, Spiritualist doctrine, and social justice. It is difficult to find New England's Gothic writers dealing with these themes until the last third of the twentieth century. Stephen King's novels and the films based upon them have been criticized for featuring the "Magical Negro," whose supernatural abilities serve as the conscience and savior of the White protagonist. The term is attrib-uted to Spike Lee, and the trope of the Magical Negro is found most promin-ently in film (Okorafor-Mbachu). In "Cinethetic Racism: White Redemption and Black Stereotypes in 'Magical Negro' Films," Matthew W. Hughey argues that like the Noble Savage, endowed by his close connection to the earth with powers of healing, the stereotypical Magical Negro exists to use those powers on behalf of the White characters, often at the cost of his or her own life (564). In the essay "Eating the Other: Desire and Resistance," bell hooks calls this trend in contemporary culture "imperialist nostalgia," where the dominant culture wishes for the insights and powers of the very people whose way of life they have destroyed (25).

In several works, Stephen King does engage with New England's history of racism, most notably in *Bag of Bones* (1998), whose Black ghost nearly destroys the White protagonist. The novel fits Brogan's definition of cul-tural haunting: "The past that resists integration into the present because it is incomprehensible or too horrific takes shape as a ghost that can possess" ("American"). The ghost in *Bag of Bones* is Sara Tidwell, the African American blues singer whose rape and murder are too horrific for the White residents of an unincorporated territory in the Maine woods (the TR) to comprehend, and so she becomes an embodied ghost who possesses the trees, the lake, and the living descendants of the men who perpetrated the outrage.

Joe Citro's *The Unseen* pits White Vermonters against what they believe to be folkloric monsters—Sasquatch, the Wendigo—until they are revealed as descendants of escaped slaves and allowed to tell their own stories. Citro denies that the novel has a historical basis—in fact, he wrote to me that Vermont is the only New England state without a record of legal slavery. He says the inspiration for *The Gore* (his preferred title for the novel) lay in "the trappings of the Underground Railroad [...] concealed passageways, hidden rooms, secrets. [...] Throw in a castle—the deserted stone hotel—and we have Vermont Gothic!"

New England still awaits an African American writer who will use the Gothic mode to confront the region's legacy of racial prejudice through cul-tural haunting, to deconstruct Hawthorne or Melville's menacing Blackness and problematic Whiteness or the trope called by Wester "blackened evil that torments and is defeated by good whiteness" (*African* 2). One candidate is

Northampton novelist, theater artist, and Smith professor Andrea Hairston whose *Redwood and Wildfire* (2011) though not set in New England deals with lynchings, the Jim Crow laws, and other injustices through African American arts and magical realism. She has told me that her forthcoming novels *will* draw on Massachusetts's Gothic history.

In 2020 New England's skeleton-filled closets opened as states, cities, universities, and families began to acknowledge their role in New England's centuries of legal slavery during and after the protests set off by the murders of George Floyd and Breonna Taylor by police. While other parts of the United States saw violent counter-protests, New England's residents for the most part expressed sympathy and solidarity for the assertion that Black Lives Matter.[1] The smallest state in the Union once had the longest name, "the State of Rhode Island and Providence Plantations." In November 2020, citizens of the state voted to drop the words "Providence Plantations." Rhode Island's Governor Raimondo said, "We cannot ignore the ugly role that slavery played in our country's history, but we can determine our state's future. This victory marks an important step in our ongoing fight to address the systemic racism that has plagued our state and our nation for centuries" (qtd. in Nunes). A prior attempt in 2010 was defeated. What had changed? The year 2020 saw icons of colonialism toppling—literally and figuratively. After centuries of denial, the Gothic secrets of slavery and racism in New England were being revealed. Protests and lawsuits at the Ivy League universities resulted in Brown, Harvard, and Yale acknowledging the role slavery played in their origins; though none are paying reparations, all are studying the issue. As Brown's Center for the Study of Slavery and Justice states, "Slavery's legacy directly impacts all of our lives, yet is 'hidden in plain sight'" ("Center").

Gothic Revivals and New England's Decline

> The Goths [...] are the noblest branch of the Caucasian race. We are their children.
> —George Perkins Marsh, "The Goths in New England" (1843)

We usually associate revivals of Gothic medievalism with the American South, where antebellum Virginia Cavaliers exemplified what Mark Twain called "The Walter Scott disease," and the Knights and Wizards of the Ku Klux Klan exemplified a less Romantic medievalist disease. Yet Gothic medievalism thrived in New England.

---

1. See *Rhode Island Slave History*; Martin; Stannard.

The 1840s began waves of Gothic revival in American vernacular architecture. The house in Grant Wood's painting is one such Carpenter Gothic creation. In New England, these multistory angular constructions with stained glass and pointed arches in wood became the icon of the haunted house. This may be because they went out of style and were abandoned, turned into rooming houses or the first "funeral parlors," and thus acquired the reputation of being haunted. This is the style of Mark Twain's home in Hartford, where he wrote *A Connecticut Yankee in King Arthur's Court* (1889). Satirically anti-medievalist, this novel became part of America's Arthurian boom of the 1890s. The Whiteness and purity of Arthur's court's association with the Anglo-Saxon race may have inspired Vermont's King Arthur Flour, which boasts of its White purity though "never bleached."

In the nineteenth century the descendants of the Puritans, who were themselves concerned with their region's constant Fall from Grace, worried that the inexorable westward march of America's Manifest Destiny could mean that their home region was no longer the hub of the universe. Marsh "the True Goth" accepts as inevitable the decline of his homeland, whose rocky farms cannot compete with those of the West and South, predicting accurately that New England will be the schoolmaster to those regions that supplant it in political power (39). Late nineteenth-century journalists lamented that rural New England had become a backwater because its fittest population had abandoned its stony farms for the fertile fields of the Midwest and West. New England's iconic stone walls are silent witnesses to the abandonment of farming: European settlers had multiplied and filled up the land that yielded in return fine crops of stones, leading to waves of westward migration searching for more fertile, less stony ground. The stone "fences" that once separated neighbors' fields became mysterious artifacts in the second-growth woods. The abandoned farmhouses became the sites of horror so cherished by Lovecraft. Seen in this light, Frost's "Mending Wall" (1914) seems Gothic with its neighbor like a Stone Age savage: "He moves in darkness as it seems to me, / Not of woods only and the shade of trees" (*North* 11). In his darkness, he will not question the saying of his fathers that "good fences make good neighbors."

The early twentieth-century eugenics movement studied those who had remained on their farms and in isolated villages and were horrified at the results, characterizing families as inbred or racial mongrels. The theory of "degenerate families" attempted to explain how sturdy Anglo-Saxon stock had yielded such pathetic specimens. Studies in Massachusetts (Danielson and Davenport) and Vermont (Gallagher) "proved" the heritability of insanity, criminal behavior, promiscuity, and alcoholism. Proponents of "negative eugenics" argued that the unfit were not only an economic burden but that left alone they would outbreed the more fit. They asked, "Can steps be taken to strike at the root of the trouble and prevent the propagation of inevitable dependents?" (Danielson and Davenport 33). Henry Perkins's Vermont Eugenics Survey succeeded in their negative eugenic goal: the Vermont legislature in 1931 passed a law requiring sterilization of the "feeble-minded" and others considered unfit. Joe Citro reworks this theme of Vermont degeneracy in the short story "Them Bald-Headed Snays" (1989). The Snays at first seem like Eugenics Survey degenerates, pale with sparse hair and little sign of intelligence. The story's child protagonist learns that the Snays are born victims who—like the poor—are always with us. His grandfather beats one such scapegoat to death and is restored to health. This disturbing parable reminds us not only of the eugenicists' attitude toward the rural poor but also of universal examinations of the problem of human pain such as Dostoevsky's "The Grand Inquisitor" or Ursula K. Le Guin's "Those Who Walk Away from Omelas."

Thanks to widespread media coverage, the popular image of New England's villages and farms included those inbred, incestuous, and sinister characters. Eugene O'Neill's *Desire under the Elms* (1924) and Edith Wharton's *Ethan Frome* (1911) and *Summer* (1917) exemplify these regional characteristics through non-supernatural examinations of backwoods isolation, thwarted and unnatural passions, twisted lives, and the consequences of guilt. In her autobiography *A Backward Glance* (1934), Wharton describes the origin of the two novels based on her trips to "grim places, [...] insanity, incest and slow mental and moral starvation were hidden away behind the paintless wooden house-fronts of the long village street, or in the isolated farm-houses on the neighbouring hills." These "grim places" were villages of Western Massachusetts only a few miles away from the summer homes of rich New Yorkers.

Some observers found conditions even worse in the cities. Boston Brahmin Charles Eliot Norton in 1905 wrote a nostalgic sketch of "old Cambridge," praising its "pure New England type" of residents some seventy years earlier, when "the progress of democracy had not swept away the natural distinctions of good breeding and superior culture" (17), sounding the racialist notes Lovecraft would echo 20 years later. Norton lamented that his beloved village of Ashfield in western Massachusetts had lost its young people to the West or to the cities, which were overrun by immigrants, Jews, and Italians. Henry James in *The American Scene* (1907) is shocked to find an Italian immigrant in Salem who knows nothing of Hawthorne or the House of the Seven Gables. Lovecraft also notes these immigrants in "Dreams in the Witch House" (1932), his only completed examination of the New England witch belief; though he told some of his many correspondents that he planned to write a novel about the Salem trials, he never did so.

Fears that rural New England had become a decayed, superstitious backwater seemed to find confirmation in newspaper coverage in 1892 of strange happenings in a graveyard in Exeter, Rhode Island. Classified until the 1990s as folklore or fiction, archaeological evidence from an abandoned graveyard in Griswold, Connecticut, has confirmed that bodies were exhumed and mutilated to prevent them from returning to prey upon the living; horrified newspaper reporters tagged this apotropaic practice with the name of the Eastern European vampire. In 1896, anthropologist George Stetson defined this "animistic vampire belief": "rural New Englanders believed that consumption is not a physical but a spiritual disease, obsession, or visitation; that as long as the body of a dead consumptive relative has blood in the heart it is proof that an occult influence steals from it for death and is at work draining the blood of the living" (3). Stetson blames the inhabitants of Exeter, who live in "isolation [...] where thought stagnates and insanity and the superstition are prevalent" (10). He cites the abandonment of farms and houses as evidence for the survival of such "superstitions of a much lower culture" (8). In this, Stetson was following the prevailing paradigm in anthropology, E. B. Tylor's "Doctrine of Survivals," which states, "On the strength of these survivals, it becomes possible to declare that the civilization of the people they are observed among must have been derived from an earlier state" (Tylor 64).[2]

New England's "animistic vampire" tradition has not often inspired the region's writers of Gothic horror. Lovecraft mentions the "Exeter superstition" (*AMM* 245) in "The Shunned House" (1924). Several women authors are exceptions: Mary Wilkins Freeman's protagonist in her short story "Luella Miller" (1902) is a living woman who sucks the life force out of everyone who loves or serves her. The villagers' belief in her vampiric power is deemed "a survival of the wild horror and frenzied fear of their ancestors" (305). Amy Lowell's narrative poem "A Dracula of the Hills" (1923) does not retell any of the known accounts but reflects many details of the native belief. Her New England hill-woman narrator addresses someone like Stetson, who has come to collect "old New England customs and beliefs":

Yes, I can understan' ther's a sort o' pleasure collectin' old customs

[...]

Superstition you call it—but I don't know.

(A. Lowell 173)

---

2. For the New England vampire belief, see Bell, *Food*; Ringel, *New*, chapter 6.

The narrator relates her observations of the passionate Florella, who, while dying of consumption, invokes the devil and proclaims her determination to live. She returns from the dead to drain the life of a willing victim, her husband. After his death, the villagers apply the traditional remedy and discover that "her heart was as fresh as a livin' person's. / Father said it glittered like a garnet" (A. Lowell 184). The poem concludes:

Oh, they burnt it; they al'ays do in such cases.
Nobody's safe till it's burnt.
Now, sir, will you tell me how such things used to be?
(A. Lowell 185)

Edith Wharton might have read this poem, for her chilly New England Gothic tale "Bewitched" (1926) also concerns a sexualized revenant who vows to come back from the dead, though in this case the return is read as witchcraft. Set in a desolate house built in an abandoned mountain village in "that lonely stretch between North Ashmore and Cold Corners," Ora Brand has "bewitched" a married man and is draining his life. His wife argues for the traditional remedy: "A stake through the breast. That's the old way; and it's the only way." But Wharton does not opt for a supernatural explanation. She has the girl's father shoot his other daughter, whose death is explained as pneumonia. The father remains convinced that he has killed the revenant Ora: "Better here than in the churchyard. They shan't dig her up *now*."[3]

The sole physical evidence for the practice of exhuming suspected revenants emerged in 1990, when Connecticut state archaeologist Dr. Nicholas Bellantoni excavated what had been the Walton family cemetery in Griswold, abandoned when that family moved West. One anomalous burial had been broken into postmortem, the rib bones disturbed, and the skull removed and reoriented. The initials "J.B." were found on the remnants of the coffin; tests at the time confirmed that he suffered from tuberculosis. Recently, DNA testing and genealogical research have yielded a possible identification of the putative vampire.[4] Writers have begun to utilize this folk medical practice and Gothic survival in fiction. Former Rhode Island resident Caitlín R. Kiernan's *The Red Tree* (2009) portrays the state's vampire outbreaks, inbred towns, and disreputable inhabitants, while the Exeter vampire Mercy Brown joins more recent blood cultists in Kiernan's short story "So Runs the World Away" (2001). Current Rhode Islander Christa Carmen's forthcoming novel *Because*

3. See Elbert, "Wharton's," for comparisons with Hawthorne's "Ethan Brand" beyond the similar names; emphasis in original.
4. See Ofgang and Daniels-Higginbotham et al. for recent discoveries.

I Could Not Stop for Death is told from Mercy's point of view. Vermont playwright Jeanne Beckwith's one-act play "The Rhode Island Chapter" provides a surprising spin on the New England vampire belief, by incorporating the trope of achieving physical immortality usually associated with the alchemists.

Better-known vampire narratives set in New England have imported their monsters directly from the European Gothic tradition. *Dark Shadows* (1966–71), the television soap opera combining monsters with the Domestic Gothic, is set in Maine, though it was filmed in Newport, Rhode Island. Stephen King's survey of horror in fiction and other media, *Danse Macabre* (1983), dismisses the importance of *Dark Shadows* (232), but perhaps readers were prepared by this popular daytime series to accept the Old World vampires King brought to Maine in *Salem's Lot* (1975). King informed me a few years after the publication of his novel that he had never heard of the existence of a New England vampire belief. Charles L. Grant's *Soft Whisper of the Dead* (1981) also imports a European vampire to his Oxrun Station. Grant told me that like King he had not known about the local belief: he chose the northwestern corner of Connecticut to set his weird fiction because of the wealthy, suburban associations of the region, not because it was the location of Connecticut's most notorious abandoned village, cursed Dudleytown.

The cycle of abandonment continued in the twentieth century, with some farms transformed into subdivisions while others returned to woodlands. Manufacturing also left New England. By the 1930s, urban industries that had attracted women from farms and immigrants from Europe began to leave for the nonunionized South. Industrial cities like Fall River, Massachusetts, and Pawtucket, Rhode Island, and regions like northeastern Connecticut and the Merrimack River valley seemed left behind by history. The abandoned factory joined the abandoned farm as proof of New England's decline and insularity. Through the medium of Gothic fiction, a generation of northeastern regionalists have objectified the spiritual malaise that accompanies such a loss of influence. Don D'Ammassa, Bracken MacLeod, Paul Tremblay, Rick Hautala, Joe Citro, Christopher Golden, Joe Hill, and many other New England horror regionalists continue the tradition of drawing on the Gothic legends and history of the area for their fiction.

Stephen King escaped the dead-end jobs of working-class Maine. One of his earliest short stories, "Graveyard Shift" (1970), exposes the horrors of a textile mill based on one where he worked whose rats and pollution are nothing compared to the Lovecraftian monsters in the subbasement. Fiction has become the King family business, with his wife's, Tabitha King's, and his sons Owen's and Joe's supernatural and psychological horror novels. The latter publishes as Joe Hill, having proved that he could succeed on his own merits rather than his father's fame. Rick Hautala, King's classmate at the University of Maine, also grew up poor. His novel *Dark Silence* (1992) is set in a sawmill on Maine's cursed Saco River, "a weathered, gray hulk that stood out against the sky like an ancient, brooding castle" (28) haunted by the apparition of a hanged witch. In Hautala's novel *Moon Walker* (1989), zombies in the Maine potato fields are walking objective correlatives for the decline of rural New England. As one of his characters notes, "A dead town! Wasn't that what she had called it ever since she could remember?" (284). Rhode Island writer and critic of science fiction and horror, Don D'Ammassa has told me that the supernatural in his fiction is both real and "a metaphor for the way all New England has been dying." His short story "Little Evils" (1991) equates corporate and supernatural ills. It is set in Taunton, Massachusetts, where D'Ammassa once worked in an abandoned mill complex, "elderly, brick faced [...] victim of the failing economy of the Northeast" (89). These horror writers do not descend from "old New England stock." Their working-class parents and grandparents were the very immigrants that Lovecraft blamed for the region's decline.

Lovecraft, His Monsters, and His Critics

I AM PROVIDENCE
—Inscribed on Lovecraft's monument, Swan Point Cemetery, Providence, Rhode Island

We Are Lovecraft's Country
—Headline, *Saturday Evening Post*, August 2020

H. P. Lovecraft was the heir to an elegiac view of New England's past. Like Hawthorne, he saw the horrors of his Puritan heritage of religious persecution and the witch belief, yet he glorified his Anglo-Saxon ancestry. He projected his fears of regional decline outward upon immigrants and degenerate cultists who worship and interbreed with aliens. His Gothic science fiction is set in an invented New England landscape and dialect that owe much to the women's tradition of local color regionalism. His materialist cosmology sets human evil and monsters against the infinite spaces of an inimical universe. As S. T. Joshi, Boswell to his Johnson, puts it, Lovecraft is responsible for "the transformation of all New England into a locus of both wonder and terror" (*Case* 235).

Following his death in 1937, Lovecraft moved from the margins of pulp fiction to become the inspiration for writers as diverse as Joyce Carol Oates, Neil Gaiman, and Stephen King; the cynosure of French- and Spanish-language critics, who hailed him as a master second only to Poe; and the object of abhorrence by contemporary readers. Lovecraft was immersed in amateur journalism, progenitor of today's online world of blogs and social media; he lived through letters to his many friends and disciples. His abridged *Selected Letters* fill five volumes: the collected letters may run to 25. Lovecraft's encouragement of friends and fans to add to his pantheon of gods and monsters and set stories in his universe shaped today's close interaction of expectations and attitudes between fans and authors in the fantastic genres. This was the original fanfiction. Publication in mass market paperback in the 1960s brought Lovecraft out of obscurity; today he is part of the Library of America. Once scorned by academic critics, today Lovecraft is seen as central to the American Gothic canon.[5]

Lovecraft's universe encompassed an imagined New England of invented towns: Arkham, home of Miskatonic University, whose library holds forbidden texts such as the *Necronomicon*; Innsmouth, a fishing port further gone in decay than Sarah Orne Jewett's Dunnet Landing; Dunwich, an inland Massachusetts village of inbred families and abandoned farms and churches. Stories set in them include "The Dunwich Horror" (1928) and "The Shadow over Innsmouth" (1931). He also set stories in Boston—"Pickman's Model"(1926)— and Southern Vermont—"The Whisperer in Darkness"(1930)—and of course witch-haunted Salem—"The Unnamable"(1923), which was inspired by Hawthorne and Mather. Superimposed on this region is his invented cosmology of gods and monsters, indescribable though vividly corporeal. "The Call of Cthulhu" (1926) introduces this tentacled undersea entity, another vision of Leviathan. Lovecraft's materialist philosophy mocks the primitive cultists who worship these invaders from other planets and dimensions as gods.

His fears of change and decay made Lovecraft a historic preservationist before the term was invented. His Anglophilia was expressed in his pose as an eighteenth-century gentleman. Steeped in the history and legends of New England and in his predecessors in the Gothic, his letters and stories juxtapose rhapsodic visions of sunset terraces and white steepled churches with nameless horrors crawling beneath. *The Case of Charles Dexter Ward* (1927; published posthumously) is Lovecraft's Gothic travelogue of Rhode Island's secret history mingling fact—the alchemists of seventeenth-century New London and Cambridge, the slave traders who led the revolution, the mental hospital where his parents died—with his outsider entities. Through obsessive genealogical research, the title character discovers a previously unknown ancestor Joseph Curwen, a necromancer and alchemist. There really was a circle of alchemists in seventeenth-century Connecticut led by John Winthrop Jr., who founded a "New" London as an alchemical colony, according to Connecticut state historian Walter Woodward's *Prospero's America*. Winthrop and Jonathan

---

5. See Ringel, *New* 157–201; Joshi's biography *I Am Providence: The Life and Times of H. P. Lovecraft*; Joshi's survey of *Four Decades of Criticism*; Evans; Houellebecq.

Brewster, son of Plymouth Colony's founder, studied alchemy at Harvard. These practitioners of "natural magic" may have inspired Hawthorne's Roger Chillingworth in *The Scarlet Letter*. The epigraph to *The Case of Charles Dexter Ward* cites Mather's *Magnalia*, a tome Lovecraft had inherited from his grandfather. Mather does make it seem as though he had personally experimented with resurrecting people from their ashes: "and by the lyke Method from the essential Saltes of humane Dust, a Philosopher may, without any criminal Necromancy, call up the Shape of any dead Ancestour from the Dust whereinto his Bodie has been incinerated" (1: 165). Lovecraft's unnatural Puritan survivals are vanquished by science.

Though Lovecraft idealized his Anglo-Saxon race, he had no difficulty condemning the Puritans who settled New England. They are his stand-ins for the monks and Inquisitors of the British Gothic revival.[6] "The Unnamable" is set in the seventeenth century, when

> there was no beauty; no freedom—we can see that from the architectural and household remains, and the poisonous sermons of the cramped divines. And inside that rusted iron strait-jacket lurked gibbering hideousness, perversion, and diabolism. (*Dagon* 203)

Lovecraft's Gothic Puritans are proof that he could hate his own race as much as he hated other races.

Lovecraft's racialist "science" had deep roots in New England. Louis Agassiz, founder of the Harvard Museum of Comparative Zoology, championed earlier theories of polygenesis (the separate creation of the races) and skull measurement to prove White European superiority. His protégé Nathaniel Shaler taught future leaders including Theodore Roosevelt the same brand of "Anglo-Saxon chauvinism" (Painter 199–200). The novella *Hottentots* (1995) by Paul Di Filippo, native Rhode Islander and prolific writer of all genres of the fantastic, is a serious romp through this lesser-known corner of New England's history, blending the real Agassiz with Mark Twain's Heaven-storming Captain Stormfield, the Hottentot Venus with Lovecraft's Innsmouth, Melville, and the Great Sea Serpent. Di Filippo concludes that "Agassiz could not foresee that [...] Charles Darwin was at work on a book called *The Origin of Species* [...] rendering Agassiz in his old age a cranky, outmoded, derided fossil himself" (236). Despite being exploded as science, Agassiz's racialist theories continued to attract disciples.

Long before Hitler, the racist "science" of eugenics dominated American thought. Then president Theodore Roosevelt feared "race suicide"; his address to the National Congress of Mothers in 1905 made it clear that he

---

6. See Ringel, "Diabolists."

was referring to Nordic Americans when he said that "a race that practiced race suicide" by having two or fewer children per person "would thereby conclusively show that it was unfit to exist" (85). At the time, some blamed the perceived low birth rate among the descendants of the Puritans on women's rights advocates or the overeducation of upper-class women who refused to do their duty to their race. Still others like Francis Walker blamed the immigrants who were "replacing" the "old New England stock" (644). Decades later, Kenneth Roberts, known for historical novels glorifying America's colonial past, echoed Walker's words. Following the First World War, Roberts predicted that unless immigration were controlled, "shoals of foreigners" would arrive ("Plain" 22). Their "alien racial differences" would drag down America's Anglo-Saxons, or else they would intermarry and form a dangerous "composite race" ("Plain" 21). Roberts's popular columns were collected in *Why Europe Leaves Home* (1922); he concludes that "the people who are coming to America are [...] unassimilatable, undesirable, and incapable of grasping American ideals" (49). He calls these immigrants "peculiar and alien" (*Why* 53). Roberts praises Lothrop Stoddard, whose theories of *The Rising Tide of Color* were lampooned by F. Scott Fitzgerald in *The Great Gatsby*. Madison Grant's *The Passing of the Great Race* (1916) went through many editions into the 1930s. These White supremacists agree that "races can not be cross-bred without mongrelization, any more than breeds of dogs" (Roberts, *Why* 22). In "Whose Country Is This?" (1921), then vice president Calvin Coolidge writes of "advancing hordes of aliens" and warns mothers who read *Good Housekeeping* that "the unassimilated alien child menaces our children" (109). His basic assumptions are those of Grant and Stoddard: "Quality of mind and body suggests that observance of ethnic law [separation of races and ethnic groups] is as great a necessity to a nation as immigration law" (14).

Lovecraft's letters from New York where he lived for a few years in the mid-1920s echo this xenophobic language. His fiction takes Roberts and Coolidge literally: his waves of "peculiar and alien" invaders are alien to Planet Earth. In "The Shadow out of Time" (1936), he gives Grant's name "The Great Race" to the most successful off-planet invaders. In this Gothic science fiction story, a Miskatonic University professor from Whittier's birthplace "of wholesome old Haverhill stock" (*DH* 370) is abducted by the time-and-space traveling aliens of the Great Race. In our world, the White supremacists went further than Lovecraft: they convinced Congress to slam the Golden Door and restrict immigration along racial lines, with quotas that would deny Jews refuge from the Holocaust.

Lovecraft's characters are always on the brink of dissolution, devolution, and madness: his fears were based on his family history as much as the theories of the eugenics movement. Lovecraft saw himself as the last of his line;

in Danvers, he visited descendants of an old family and described the sight in a letter (May 1, 1923): "In the veins of those terrible wrecks—last of their line—flows the mingled blood of all that was proudest. [...] Such is the dying New-England of today" (*SL* 1: 220). Lovecraft and his friends championed the Vermont laws mandating sterilization of the "unfit," some of whom were Native American or of mixed race. In "The Whisperer in Darkness," Lovecraft sets forth what has since become a cliché: alien abduction. The narrator wonders if the monstrous bodies found after the Great Vermont Flood of 1927 could be the inbred descendants of the families demonized by the Vermont Eugenics Survey: "After all, there might be some queer and perhaps hereditarily misshapen outcasts in those shunned hills" (*DH* 220). Instead, they are monsters from outer space: Vermont's hills are mined by alien winged crab things. And worse outsiders than these await the protagonist in an old farmhouse. Lovecraft's fears of mongrelization, of miscegenation producing monstrous births can be seen in "The Shadow over Innsmouth" and other stories of humans mating with monsters.

The publication of Lovecraft's amateur writings and correspondence has made readers aware of the racist opinions that are treated allegorically in his fiction. Recently, this aspect of his reputation has received the most media attention. Nnedi Okorafor, Daniel Jose Older, and other writers of color in the fantastic genres condemned Lovecraft's racism, resulting in the removal in 2016 of his image, a caricature bust by Gahan Wilson, from the World Fantasy Award (Okorafor; Flood). This affray reminds us that the "reception" of the Gothic is more than a metaphor, that the dead hand of the past, like the falling helmet of the *Castle of Otranto*, has an impact on the present.

While Lovecraft continues to inspire fans and imitators, each year brings more oppositional responses to Lovecraft's oeuvre. Matt Ruff's *Lovecraft Country* (2016) reveals New England's record of racial injustice. In 2020 this metafiction became an HBO series produced by Jordan Peele, the director of *Get Out*, whose showrunner is Misha Green, an African American woman. This creative team brought Lovecraft and America's Gothic racial secrets to a much wider audience (as noted by the *Saturday Evening Post* in the epigraph to this section). Ruff's novel and its television adaptation reverse Lovecraft's polarities: the heroic protagonists are Black, while the evil sorcerers are Nordic types. Both versions deconstruct the stereotypes of Black characters in horror fiction and film. In the novel, one woman, a medium, questions the trope of the Magical Negro:

White folks' belief that Negroes were magically gifted struck her as the most absurd form of superstition. Sorcery was in the Bible, which meant it was real, but [...] like every other kind of power it would be concentrated in the hands of the mighty. A *real* magician would almost surely be a white man, most likely the sort whose ancestors went around in powdered wigs. (Ruff 220–21; emphasis in original)

The heroes of *Lovecraft Country* publish *The Safe Negro's Travel Guide*, a version of the actual *Green Book* that listed accommodations catering to African American travelers under segregation. To resolve the novel (though not the television adaptation), the heroes put the sorcerer Braithwhite under the same sort of travel restrictions. Braithwhite threatens them with the wrath of remaining cultists, and Atticus Freeman responds: "What is it you're trying to scare me with? You think I don't know what country I live in? I know. We all do. We always have. *You're* the one who doesn't understand" (Ruff 366; emphasis in original). Aired during the pandemic soon after the height of the Black Lives Matter protests, the television series may have shown viewers looking for escape that the best horror reflects and comments upon reality.

Victor LaValle's award-winning novella *The Ballad of Black Tom* (2016) performs the same type of reversal on one of Lovecraft's most racist and xenophobic stories, "The Horror at Red Hook" (1927). LaValle told an interviewer that he intended to continue Lovecraft's legacy of encouraging "fanfiction of his own stories to overwrite that legacy into newer, more progressive visions of horror" (qtd. in Romano). LaValle's novella questions Lovecraft's assumption that the ultimate horror is a universe indifferent to man; instead, the characters of *The Ballad of Black Tom* see

the police forces at the barricades as they muscled the crowd of Negroes back [...] the patrol cars. [...] What was indifference compared to malice?

"Indifference would be such a relief!" (LaValle 66)

Black Tom is a conflicted antihero: the story is in dialogue not only with Lovecraft but also with Richard Wright's *Native Son* and Ralph Ellison's *Invisible Man*. For both Ruff and LaValle, placing Black men at the center of their responses to Lovecraft foregrounds the everyday racist threats of lynching and police violence faced by the protagonists, which make the monsters and demons less horrifying by contrast. As Black Tom says to the police, "I'll take Cthulhu over you devils any day" (LaValle 143).

Ruthanna Emrys's Innsmouth Legacy novels respond to the racialist fears of Lovecraft's "The Shadow over Innsmouth" by taking the point of view of his monstrous Deep Ones, transforming them into the displaced, persecuted immigrants for which they were Lovecraft's metaphor. She addresses many of Lovecraft's problematics for modern readers: misogyny and the erasure of women, xenophobia, and White supremacy. Her novels form an alternate history of the United States and Lovecraft's imagined New England. Also confronting perceptions of Lovecraft's misogyny and racism are two ground-breaking women's anthologies from 2015: *Dreams from the Witch House: Female Voices of Lovecraftian Horror*, edited by Lynne Jamneck; and *She Walks in Shadows*, edited by Silvia Moreno-Garcia and Paula R. Stiles, including stories by Caitlin R. Kiernan, Sonya Taaffe, and many other new voices in New England's Gothic literature.

Not all current responses to Lovecraft are adversarial: video and live-action roleplaying games based on his mythos remain popular, and pastiches and novels that accept his pantheon and his assumptions continue to be published. Massachusetts writer Douglas Wynne's *Red Equinox* and its two sequels are set in an alternate postapocalyptic timeline where Lovecraft's places, cultists, and monsters are everyday fact, with the supersecret agency SPECTRA pitted against or experimenting with these threats. Wynne explains that he uses Lovecraft's universe, minus the misogyny and racism, "as a commentary on issues like climate change, the techno-surveillance state, and the war on terrorism, because the paranoid xenophobia and fear of insignificance that define so much of Lovecraft's work are just as alive today in the era of Fox News as they were in the 1930s."

In our timeline, Gothic horror filmed in New England tends to rely upon clichés—cursed Indian burial grounds, haunted houses, psychic investigators. By contrast, Robert Eggers's *The Witch: A New-England Folktale* (2015) exists within a seventeenth-century mindset, embodying the ecophobia and wilder-ness Gothic of its 1630s setting even to an attempt at period language: the film does not explain away its magic. The animated children's film *ParaNorman* (2012) presents a surprisingly nuanced response to the New England witch belief and its modern consequences. The same Gothic Puritans that Lovecraft so reviled are at its heart; more traditionally Gothic than most adult films, *ParaNorman* features Byronic heroes, inescapable ancestral curses, and a landscape of dilapidated houses. This film is part of the thriving genre of "KinderGoth," which has spawned tentacled plush toys and Lovecraftian children's alphabet books (Ringel and Randall).

Attracting the most critical attention, Peele's *Get Out* deconstructs the roles of Black characters in horror film while reflecting the realities of race in America. Peele's mad-scientist device of a process that steals Black bodies to allow Whites to prolong their consciousness inside them makes literal bell hooks's concept of "Eating the Other." Maisha Wester notes the parallels with Ira Levin's *The Stepford Wives*, also set in the Connecticut suburbs:

In a film without supernatural monsters, horror is complexly relocated within black bodies at very specific moments, alluding to how blacks have been historically marked as monstrous in social discourses and (Gothic) fictions while clarifying the moments when blacks actually become monstrous—the moment when they become Stepford blacks. ("Black Diasporic" 303)

Elizabeth Patton links the film with Loewen's sundown towns, making the point that Peele deliberately set it in the Northeast to differentiate *Get Out* from the more familiar Jim Crow South setting. Alison Landsberg calls this type of cinema, which accomplishes political work using the conventions of the horror movie, "truthful": in her genre of "horror vérité the terrifying night-mare is everyday reality" (632).

In the visual arts, the icon for New England Gothic is the haunted mansion in the Carpenter Gothic style associated with Charles Addams; every town has its old witch house, abandoned mill, or ruined farmhouse. Even such post-card scenes as ancient graveyards, the sea, covered bridges, and stone walls inspire horror in the works of painters Alan Clark and Duncan Eagleson. The long-running comic book series *Swamp Thing*, though set in Louisiana, was drawn for years by native Vermonters Steve Bissette and Rick Veitch, and according to Bissette, "the landscapes that come out of my fingers are very much Vermont." Joe Hill and Chilean artist Gabriel Rodriguez created the comic book series *Locke & Key*, begun in 2008 and continuing today in graphic novel collections and as a Netflix series. From the first story arc "Welcome to Lovecraft," the series advertises its New England Gothic inspiration. The town of Lovecraft, Massachusetts, has family curses, Revolutionary War secrets, and adventures through time and space for its teenage and child protagonists.

It (1986), Stephen King's compendium of horrors, seems to touch upon every trope of the New England Gothic: Puritan guilt, fear of the wilderness, sins of the fathers, secret histories, ghosts, and folk horror. "It" is the monster with a thousand faces, with Pennywise the Clown the most (in)famous. Like Lovecraft's god-monsters, It comes from alien dimensions to Derry, King's version of his home, Bangor, Maine: "It's become a part of Derry. [...] Only It's not a matter of outward geography [...] now It's ... inside. Somehow It's gotten inside" (503). "It" is the monster who scares us and the monster who *is* us, the Outsider and the Insider. King deals explicitly with Maine's history of racism: the book is narrated by Mike Hanlon, an African American who expe-rienced prejudice growing up in Derry. His father taught him about lynchings and the 1930 attack of a Klan-like group, the Legion of White Decency, on a Negro soldiers' club. Unlike many of the book's folkloric hauntings, this event does not appear to have a historical basis, but the racist attitudes of the White people of "America's whitest state" are accurately reflected, as are the sufferings of their victims. Worst of all, the arson at "The Black Spot" is perpetrated not by supernatural monsters but by the citizens of Derry, and afterward, like the slave owners, Indian killers, and witch accusers of New England's past, they forget about what they had done. The dead past does not stay dead when writers turn to the Gothic mode to reveal crimes and secret shame.

Like the Puritans who crowded into the haunted chambers of Mather's possessed girls and bought his accounts of horrors and wonders, today's readers continue to seek out the dangerous delights of the Gothic. Tales of monsters, witches, and the undead remain a reliable New England export, even when other manufacturing enterprises of the region have failed. Salem is the "Halloween Capital" of America, and Gothic tourism thrives in New England—or will do once the real-life horrors of COVID-19 have subsided. Paul Tremblay's *Survivor Song* (2020), written before the pandemic, is apocalyptic Gothic horror in a cozy suburban Massachusetts setting, full circle from Jonathan Edwards. The Gothic adapts well to end times and paranoia, though real life persists in outstripping the monsters of fiction and film. The electronic reality in which we live is visualized as a haunted wood of ghosts and trolls or a World Wide Web spun by monstrous spiders. In their introduction to *Twenty-First Century Gothic*, Wester and Reyes note that "the Gothic has continued to adapt to contemporary times [...] hybridising further to the point where an engagement with the tradition's origins has been complicated by the postmodern simulacral recuperation of the mode and its multifarious monsters" (13). The monsters who scare us, who *are* us.

Can there be a happy ending to New England's often-tragic Gothic story? Can the dead find rest, the living find peace? Stephen King thinks so—even his most apocalyptic monster jamboree *The Mist* ends with the word "hope" (492). Or as his stand-in Bill Denbrough advises at the conclusion of *It*:

> Go toward all the life there is with all the courage you can find and all the belief you can muster. Be true, be brave, stand.
>
> All the rest is darkness. (1136)

WORKS CITED

Adams, Liz Duffy. *Wonders of the Invisible World*. The New Play Exchange, 2013, newplayexchange.org/plays/13361/wonders-invisible-world.

Alcott, Louisa May. "Transcendental Wild Oats." 1873. *Silver Pitchers: And, Independence: A Centennial Love Story*. Boston: Roberts, 1876, pp. 79–101, archive.org/details/silverpitchersan00alcouoft/page/100/mode/2up.

Babson, John J. *History of the Town of Gloucester, Cape Ann*. Gloucester: Procter Bros., 1860, www.google.com/books/edition/History_of_the_Town_of_Gloucester_Cape_A/ORhFAQAAMAAJ?hl=en&gbpv=1&bsq=Wesson.

Bacon, Josephine Dodge Daskam. "The Gospel." Lundie, pp. 235–51.

Baker, Emerson W., and James Kences. "Maine, Indian Land Speculation, and the Essex County Witchcraft Outbreak of 1692." *Maine History*, vol. 40, no. 3, 2001, pp. 158–89, digitalcommons.library.umaine.edu/cgi/viewcontent.cgi?article=1197&context=mainehistoryjournal. Accessed Sep. 10, 2021.

Ballou, Adin. *History of the Hopedale Community*. Lowell, MA: Thompson & Hill, 1897, books.google.com/books?id=sXdDAAAAIAAJ&pg=PA132&dq=Northampton+Association+of+Education+and+Industry.&hl=en&newbks=1&newbks_redir=0&sa=X&ved=2ahUKEwim5NTfqZLuAhUEWs0KHaHCAxE4ChDoATABegQIARAC#v=onepage&q=Northampton%20Association&f=false.

Beckman, John. *American Fun: Four Centuries of Joyous Revolt*. Pantheon Books, 2014.

Beckwith, Jeanne. *The Rhode Island Chapter*. The New Play Exchange, 2018, newplayexchange.org/plays/197309/rhode-island-chapter.

Bell, Michael. *Food for the Dead: On the Trail of New England's Vampires*. Wesleyan UP, 2011.

———. "The Legend of the Palatine." Quahog.org, www.quahog.org/factsfolklore/index.php?id=92. Accessed Sep. 10, 2021.

Benét, Stephen Vincent. "Daniel Webster and the Sea Serpent." *Thirteen O'Clock: Stories of Several Worlds*. Farrar & Rinehart, 1937, www.fadedpage.com/books/20110501/html.php.

———. *The Devil and Daniel Webster: And Other Stories*. Arch, 1967.

Bergland, Renee L. *The National Uncanny: Indian Ghosts and American Subjects*. Dartmouth College UPNE, 2000.

Billy, Ted. "Descendentalism and the Dark Romantics: Poe, Hawthorne, Melville, and the Subversion of American Transcendentalism." Crow, pp. 151–63.

Bissette, Steve. Zoom interview. December 21, 2020.

Bissette, Stephen R. "The Gods of the Hills: *DARK AUGUST* and Vermont Folk Horror." Booklet to accompany DVD *American Horror Project Vol. 2*. Arrow Films, 2019, www.dvdbeaver.com/film2/DVDReviews38/american_horror_project_vol_2_blu-ray.htm.

Boyd, Colleen, and Coll Thrush, editors. *Phantom Past, Indigenous Presence: Native Ghosts in North American Culture and History*. U of Nebraska P, 2011.

Boyer, Paul S., and Stephen Nissenbaum, editors. *The Salem Witchcraft Papers*. 3 vols. Da Capo, 1977.

Braude, Ann. *Radical Spirits: Spiritualism and Women's Rights in Nineteenth-Century America*. Beacon, 1989.

Brockden Brown, Charles. *Edgar Huntly; or, Memoirs of a Sleepwalker*. 1799. Bicentennial Edition, edited by Sydney J. Krause and S. W. Reid, Kent State UP, 1984.

Brogan, Kathleen. "American Stories of Cultural Haunting: Tales of Heirs and Ethnographers." *Short Story Criticism*, vol. 58, edited by Janet Witalec, Gale, 2003, go-gale-com.uscga.idm.oclc.org/ps/i.do?p=LitRC&u=23266&id=GALE|H1420048623&v=2.1&it=r&sid=LitRC&asid=a0b57066.

——. *Cultural Haunting: Ghosts and Ethnicity in Recent American Literature*. UP of Virginia, 1998.

Brown, Alice. "There and Here." *High Noon*. Houghton, Mifflin, 1904, pp. 65–92, books.google.com/books?id=0voXAAAAYAAJ&newbks=1&newbks_redir=0&dq=Alice+Brown+High+Noon&source=gbs_navlinks_s.

Brownfield, Troy. "We Are Lovecraft's Country." *Saturday Evening Post*, August 19, 2020, www.saturdayeveningpost.com/2020/08/we-are-lovecrafts-country/. Accessed Sep. 10, 2021.

Buckley, C. A., and James Merrill. "Exploring *The Changing Light at Sandover*: An Interview with James Merrill." *Twentieth Century Literature*, vol. 38, no. 4, 1992, pp. 415–35, www.jstor.org/stable/441784. Accessed Sep. 10, 2021.

Burnham, Michelle. "Is There an Indigenous Gothic?" Crow, pp. 225–37.

Burr, George Lincoln. *Narratives of the Witchcraft Cases, 1648–1706*. Charles Scribner's Sons, 1914, archive.org/details/narrativeswitch03burrgoog/page/n5/mode/2up.

Calef, Robert. *Another Brand Pluck'd from the Burning, or More Wonders of the Invisible World*. Burr, pp. 289–394.

Carter, Angela. "The Fall River Axe Murders." 1981. *Burning Your Boats: The Collected Short Stories*. Penguin, 1995, pp. 300–320.

Castle, Terry. *The Apparitional Lesbian: Female Homosexuality and Modern Culture*. Columbia UP, 1993.

Caulkins, Frances Manwaring. *History of Norwich, Connecticut from Its Settlement in 1660 to January 1845*. Norwich, 1845, www.google.com/books/edition/History_of_Norwich_Connecticut/d-SOZZA4leEC?hl=en&gbpv=1.

Center for the Study of Slavery and Justice. Brown University, www.brown.edu/initiatives/slavery-and-justice/. Accessed Sep. 10, 2021.

[Chamberlayne, Richard]. *Lithobolia, or, The Stone-Throwing Devil* ... 1698, quod.lib.umich.edu/cgi/t/text/text-idx?c=eebo;idno=A31609.0001.001.

Checker, Nick, writer. "The Curse of Micah Rood." Directed by Alec Asten. Firesite Films, 2008.

Child, Lydia Maria. *An Appeal in Favor of That Class of Americans Called Africans*. Boston: Ticknor and Fields, 1833, www.google.com/books/edition/An_Appeal_in_Favor_of_That_Class_of_Amer/pePcLMnLP7IC?hl=en&gbpv=1&bsq=Africans.

——. *Hobomok*. 1824. Settler Literature Archive 7, commons.und.edu/settler-literature/7.

Citro, Joseph A. *Cursed in New England: Stories of Damned Yankees*. Globe Pequot, 2004.

——. *Dark Twilight*. Warner, 1991. Repr. as *Lake Monsters*. Hardscrabble Books/UP of New England, 2001.

——. *Passing Strange: True Tales of New England Hauntings and Horror*. Chapters, 1996.

———. *The Unseen*. Warner, 1990. Repr. as *The Gore*. Hardscrabble Books/UP of New England, 2000.

———. "Them Bald-Headed Snays." *Masques III*, edited by J. N. Williamson, St. Martin's, 1989, pp. 265–74.

Clute, John. *The Encyclopedia of Fantasy*, sf-encyclopedia.uk/fe.php?nm=taproot_texts.

Coffin, Robert P. Tristram. *John Dawn*. Macmillan, 1936, catalog.hathitrust.org/Record/000666066.

Cohen, Jeffrey Jerome, editor. *Monster Theory: Reading Culture*. U of Minnesota P, 1996.

Comstock, Sarah. "The Broomstick Trail." *Harper's Monthly Magazine*, Dec. 1919, pp. 1–13, www.unz.com/print/Harpers-1919dec-00001/.

Condé, Maryse. *I, Tituba, Black Witch of Salem*. Translated by Richard Philcox, UP of Virginia, 1992.

The Conjuring. Directed by James Wan. New Line Cinema, 2013.

The Conjuring 3: The Devil Made Me Do It. Directed by Michael Chaves. New Line Cinema, 2021.

Cooke, Rose Terry. "My Visitation." *American Gothic from Salem Witchcraft to H.P. Lovecraft: An Anthology*. 2nd ed., edited by Charles L. Crow, Wiley Blackwell, 2013, pp. 152–63.

Coolidge, Calvin. "Whose Country Is This?" *Good Housekeeping*, Feb. 1921, pp. 13+, books.google.com/books?id=2mwjAQAAMAAJ&vq=Coolidge&dq=Coolidge+Good+Housekeeping+Whose+Country+Is+This&source=gbs_navlinks_s.

Cooper, James Fenimore. *The Last of the Mohicans: A Narrative of 1757*. 3 vols. London: John Miller, 1826, books.google.com/books?id=oVNMAAAAcAAJ&source=gbs_navlinks_s.

———. *The Wept of Wish-ton-Wish: A Tale*. 1829. 2 vols. New York: Stringer and Townsend, 1852, ia801308.us.archive.org/16/items/weptwishtonwish01coopgoog/weptwishtonwish01coopgoog.pdf.

Cox, F. Brett. *The End of All Our Exploring: Stories*. Fairwood Press, 2018.

Crow, Charles L., editor. *A Companion to American Gothic*. Wiley Blackwell, 2014.

D'Ammassa, Don. "Little Evils." *Chilled to the Bone*, edited by Robert T. Garcia, Mayfair Games, 1991, pp. 87–100.

Damon, S. Foster. *The Moulton Tragedy: A Heroic Poem with Lyrics*. Gambit, 1970.

———. *Witch of Dogtown: A Drama in Three Acts*. Providence, 1955.

D'Arcy, Uriah Derick. *The Black Vampyre; A Legend of St. Domingo*. New York, 1819, Text prepared by Ed White and Duncan Faherty, jto.common-place.org/wp-content/uploads/sites/2/2019/08/Black-Vampyre-for-JTO.pdf.

Danielson, Florence H., and Charles B. Davenport. *The Hill Folk: Report on a Community of Hereditary Defectives*. Eugenics Record Office, 1912, books.google.com/books?id=qqMSAAAAYAAJ&newbks=1&newbks_redir=0&dq=Perkins+Vermont+Eugenics+Survey&source=gbs_navlinks_s.

Daniels-Higginbotham, Jennifer, et al. "DNA Testing Reveals the Putative Identity of JB55, a 19th Century Vampire Buried in Griswold, Connecticut." *Genes* (Basel), Sept. 10, 2019, pp. 636+, doi:10.3390/genes10090636.

Dark August. Directed by Martin Goldman, written by Martin Goldman and J. J. Barry. Raffia Productions, 1976.

Dark Shadows. Dan Curtis Productions. American Broadcasting Company, 1966–71.

Davison, Carol Margaret. "Getting Their Knickers in a Twist: Contesting the 'Female Gothic' in Charlotte Dacre's *Zofloya*." *Gothic Studies*, vol. 11, no. 1, 2009, pp. 32–45.

———. "Haunted House/Haunted Heroine: Female Gothic Closets in 'The Yellow Wallpaper.'" *Women's Studies*, vol. 33, no. 1, 2004, pp. 47–75, www.tandfonline.com/doi/full/10.1080/00497870490267197. Accessed Sep. 10, 2021.

Day, William Patrick. *In the Circles of Fear and Desire: A Study of Gothic Fantasy*. U of Chicago P, 1985.

Delano, Amasa. *A Narrative of Voyages and Travels in the Northern and Southern Hemispheres: Comprising Three Voyages Round the World*. Boston, 1817, www.tandfonline.com/doi/abs/10.1080/00497870490267197.

DeLucia, Christine. *Memory Lands: King Philip's War and the Place of Violence in the Northeast*. Yale UP, 2018.

DeRosa, Robin. *The Making of Salem: The Witch Trials in History, Fiction and Tourism*. McFarland, 2009.

Dickinson, Emily. *The Letters of Emily Dickinson*, edited by Theodora Van Wagenen Ward, Harvard UP, 1986.

Di Filippo, Paul. *Hottentots*. *The Steampunk Trilogy*. Four Walls Eight Windows, 1995, pp. 85–236.

East, Elyssa. *Dogtown: Death and Enchantment in a New England Ghost Town*. Free Press, 2009.

Edwards, Jonathan. *Sinners in the Hands of an Angry God. A Sermon Preached at Enfield, July 8th, 1741*. Edinburgh, 1745, www.google.com/books/edition/Sinners_in_the_hands_of_an_angry_God_A_S/aBxdAAAAcAAJ?hl=en&gbpv=1&dq=sinners+in+the+hands+of+an+angry+god&printsec=frontcover.

Elbert, Monika M. "Wharton's Hybridization of Hawthorne's 'Brand' of Gothic: Gender Crossings in 'Ethan Brand' and 'Bewitched.'" *ATQ: 19th Century American Literature and Culture*, vol. 17, no. 4, 2003, pp. 221+. Gale Literature Resource Center, link.gale.com/apps/doc/A112411582/LitRC?u=23266&sid=summon&xid=08e021b5. Accessed October, 2021.

Emerson, Ralph Waldo. "Self-Reliance." *Essays*, pp. 79–116, www.gutenberg.org/files/16643/16643-h/16643-h.htm#SELF-RELIANCE.

Emrys, Ruthanna. *Deep Roots*. Tom Doherty, 2018.

———. *Winter Tide*. Tom Doherty, 2017.

Estok, Simon C. "Theorizing in a Space of Ambivalent Openness: Ecocriticism and Ecophobia." *ISLE: Interdisciplinary Studies in Literature and Environment*, vol. 16, no. 2, 2009, pp. 203–25, doi.org/10.1093/isle/isp010. Accessed Sep. 10, 2021.

Evans, Timothy H. "A Last Defense against the Dark: Folklore, Horror, and the Uses of Tradition in the Works of H. P. Lovecraft." *Journal of Folklore Research*, vol. 42, no. 1, 2005, pp. 99–135, www.jstor.org/stable/3814792. Accessed Sep. 10, 2021.

Farber, Norma. *Mercy Short: A Winter Journal, North Boston, 1692–93*. Dutton, 1982.

Fiedler, Leslie. *Love and Death in the American Novel*. 1960. Dalkey Archive Press, 1997.

Flood, Alison. "HP Lovecraft Biographer Rages against Ditching of Author as Fantasy Prize Emblem." *Guardian*, Nov. 11, 2015. www.theguardian.com/books/2015/nov/11/hp-lovecraft-biographer-rages-against-ditching-of-author-as-fantasy-prize-emblem#:~:text=HP%20Lovecraft's%20biographer%20ST%20Joshi,worst%20sort%20of%20political%20correctness%E2%80%9D.. Accessed Sep. 10, 2021.

Forbes, Esther. *A Mirror for Witches: in which is reflected the life, machinations & death of famous Doll Bilby who with a more than feminine perversity preferred a demon to a mortal lover. Here is also told how and why a righteous and most awful judgment befel her, destroying both corporeal body & immortal soul*. Heinemann, 1928.

Freneau, Philip. "The Indian Burying Ground." *The Poems of Philip Freneau*, edited by Fred Lewis Pattee, vol. 2, University Library, 1902, pp. 369–70, rpo.library.utoronto.ca/content/indian-burying-ground.

Frost, Robert. *A Boy's Will*. Henry Holt, 1915.

———. *North of Boston*. Henry Holt, 1914.

Gallagher, Nancy L. *Breeding Better Vermonters: The Eugenics Project in the Green Mountain State*. UP of New England, 1999.

Gilbert, Sandra M., and Susan Gubar. *The Madwoman in the Attic: The Woman Writer and the Nineteenth-Century Literary Imagination*. Yale UP, 1984.

Gilman, Charlotte Perkins. "The Giant Wistaria." Lundie, pp. 123–30.

———. "In Duty Bound." *In This Our World and Other Poems*. San Francisco: James H. Barry and John H. Marble, 1895, p. 30, www.google.com/books/edition/In_this_Our_World_and_Other_Poems/Bt83AAAAYAAJ?hl=en&gbpv=1&bsq=Duty%20Bound.

———. "The Yellow Wallpaper."1892. *The Yellow Wallpaper by Charlotte Perkins Gilman*, edited by Dale M. Bauer, Bedford Cultural Editions, Bedford, 1998, pp. 41–59.

———. "Why I Wrote 'The Yellow Wallpaper.'" Bauer, pp. 348–49.

Ginsberg, Lesley. "Hawthorne's Transatlantic Gothic House of Fiction: The House of the Seven Gables." *Hawthorne's Gothic*, special issue of *Nathaniel Hawthorne Review*, vol. 38, no. 2, 2012, pp. 27–46, *JSTOR*, www.jstor.org/stable/10.5325/nathhawtrevi.38.2.0027. Accessed Sep. 10, 2021.

Goddu, Teresa A. *Gothic America: Narrative, History, and Nation*. Columbia UP, 1997.

Goldberg, Robert Alan. "Conspiracy Theories in America: A Historical Overview." *Conspiracy Theories in American History: An Encyclopedia*. Vol. 1, edited by Peter Knight, ABC-CLIO, 2003, pp. 1–11.

Goss, K. David. *The Salem Witch Trials: A Reference Guide*. ABC-CLIO, 2008.

Goudsward, David, editor. *Snowbound with Zombies: Tales of the Supernatural Inspired by the Life & Work of John Greenleaf Whittier*. Post Mortem Press, 2015.

Grant, Charles L. *The Soft Whisper of the Dead*. Donald M. Grant, Publisher, 1982.

———. "A Night of Dark Intent." *Tales from the Nightside*. Arkham House, 1981, pp. 63–73.

Grant, Madison. *The Passing of the Great Race; or, The Racial Basis of European History*. 4th ed. Scribner's, 1921, archive.org/stream/passingofgreatra00granuoft/passingofgreatra00granuoft_djvu.txt.

Gray, Roland Palmer. *Songs and Ballads of the Maine Lumberjacks: With Other Songs from Maine*. Harvard UP, 1924.

Guiney, Louise Imogen. *A Roadside Harp*. Houghton, Mifflin, 1906, catalog.hathitrust.org/Record/100481120.

Hairston, Andrea. *Redwood and Wildfire*. Aqueduct Press, 2011.

Hall, David D., editor. *Witch-hunting in Seventeenth-Century New England: A Documentary History 1638–1692*. Northeastern UP, 1991.

The Haunting in Connecticut. Directed by Peter Cornwell. Lionsgate, 2009.

Hautala, Rick. *Dark Silence*. Zebra, 1992.

———. *Moon Walker*. Zebra, 1989.

———. *Untcigahunk—the Complete Little Brothers*. E-book. 2012.

———. Personal Interview. Westbrook, Maine. 1993.

Hawthorne, Nathaniel. "Alice Doane's Appeal." *Sketches and Studies*. Boston: Houghton Mifflin, 1883, pp. 157–76, books.google.com/books?id=5WwUAQAAMAAJ&newbks=1&newbks_redir=0&printsec=frontcover#v=onepage&q&f=false.

———. *The Blithedale Romance*. 1852, edited by William E. Cain, Bedford, 1996.

———. *Dr. Grimshawe's Secret: A Romance*, edited by Julian Hawthorne, Boston: Houghton Mifflin, 1882.

————. "Egotism: or, The Bosom Serpent." *United States Magazine and Democratic Review*, vol. 12, March 1843, pp. 255–61, books.google.com/books?id=QzE4AQAAMAAJ&newbks= 1&newbks_redir=0&dq=The+United+States+Magazine+and+Democratic+ Review+March+1843&source=gbs_navlinks_s.

————. "Ethan Brand: A Chapter from an Abortive Romance." *The Snow Image and Other Twice-Told Tales*. Boston: Ticknor, Reed and Fields, 1851, pp. 102–24, books.google.com/ books?id=V_REAQAAMAAJ&newbks=1&newbks_redir=0&source=gbs_navlinks_s.

————. "Feathertop: A Moralized Legend." *Mosses from an Old Manse*. Vol. 1. Boston: Ticknor and Fields, 1854, pp. 259–86, books.google.com/books?id=6MQNAAAAQAAJ&newbks= 1&newbks_redir=0&dq=grassy+and+weed-grown+cellar&source=gbs_navlinks_s.

————. "The Hollow of the Three Hills." *Twice Told Tales*. Philadelphia: David McKay, 1889, pp. 191–96, books.google.com/books?id=PiIZAAAAYAAJ&newbks=1&newbks_ redir=0&dq=Twice+Told+Tales.+Philadelphia:+David+McKay,1889&source=gbs_ navlinks_s.

————. *The House of the Seven Gables*. Boston: Ticknor and Fields, 1851, www.google.com/ books/edition/The_House_of_the_Seven_Gables/OG4RAAAAYAAJ?q=&gbpv= 1#f=false.

————. *Letters*. Vol. 17. *Centenary Edition of the Works of Nathaniel Hawthorne*, edited by William L. Charvat, Thomas Woodson, et al., Ohio State UP, 1962.

————. "The Maypole of Merry Mount." *Twice Told Tales*. Philadelphia: David McKay, 1889, pp. 49–62, books.google.com/books?id=PiIZAAAAYAAJ&newbks=1&newbks_ redir=0&dq=Twice+Told+Tales.+Philadelphia:+David+McKay,1889&source=gbs_ navlinks_s.

————. Review of Whittier's *The Supernaturalism of New England*. Whittier, *Supernaturalism*, pp. 130–33.

————. "Roger Malvin's Burial." *The Token and Atlantic Souvenir: A Christmas and New Year's Present*. 1832, pp. 161–88, babel.hathitrust.org/cgi/pt?id=hvd.32044011233574&view= 1up&seq=25.

————. *The Scarlet Letter: A Romance*. Boston: Ticknor, Reed and Fields, 1850, books.google. com/books?id=MXk6AQAAMAAJ&source=gbs_navlinks_s.

————. "A Virtuoso's Collection." *Mosses from an Old Manse*. Vol. 2. 1854. Thomas Y. Crowell, 1900, pp. 223–45, books.google.com/books?id=YYA5AQAAMAAJ&newbks= 1&newbks_redir=0&dq=A+Virtuoso%27s+Collection&source=gbs_navlinks_s.

Hill, Joe. "Dead-Wood." *20th Century Ghosts*. William Morrow, 2007, pp. 205–6.

Hill, Joe, and Gabriel Rodriguez. *Locke & Key. Vol. 1: Welcome to Lovecraft*. IDW Publishing, 2009.

Hitchcock, Enos. *Memoirs of the Bloomsgrove Family: in a series of Letters to a Respectable Citizen of Philadelphia. Containing Sentiments on a Mode of Domestic Education, Suited to the present State of Society, Government, and Manners in the United States of America: and on the Dignity and Importance of the Female Character*. 2 vols. Boston: Thomas and Andrews, 1790.

Hoffman, Alice. *Magic Lessons*. Simon and Schuster, 2020.

————. *Practical Magic*. Putnam, 1995.

Hogle, Jerrold. "The Progress of Theory and the Study of the American Gothic." Crow, pp. 3–15.

Hogle, Jerrold, and Andrew Smith. "Revisiting the Gothic and Theory: An Introduction." *Gothic Studies*, vol. 11, no. 1, 2009, pp. 1–8.

hooks, bell. *Black Looks: Race and Representation*. South End Press, 1992.

Hopkins, Caitlin Galante-Deangelis. "The Beautiful, Forgotten and Moving Graves of New England's Slaves." *Atlas Obscura*, October 26, 2016, www.atlasobscura.com/articles/the-beautiful-and-forgotten-gravesites-of-new-englands-slaves?fbclid=IwAR1I hDk4dvxFJV5GdmMQXkemH8W3brRvMQTuBeIWaKA3ry0AMHdrXyi3Y4o. Accessed Sep. 10, 2021.

Houellebecq, Michel. *H.P. Lovecraft: Against the World, Against Life.* Translated by Dorna Khazeni, Believer Books, 2005.

Hood, Thomas. "The Haunted House: A Romance." *Hood's Magazine and Comic Miscellany*, vol. 1, no. 1, 1844, pp. 1–11.

Howe, Katharine. *The Physick Book of Deliverance Dane.* Hachette, 2009.

Howells, William Dean. *The Undiscovered Country.* Boston: Houghton, Mifflin, 1880, books. google.com/books?id=pM5aAAAAMAAJ&newbks=1&newbks_redir=0&dq=The+ Undiscovered+Country+Howells&source=gbs_navlinks_s.

Hughey, Matthew W. "Cinethetic Racism: White Redemption and Black Stereotypes in 'Magical Negro' Films." *Social Problems*, vol. 56, no. 3, 2009, pp. 543–77, doi.org/ 10.1525/sp.2009.56.3.543. Accessed Sep. 10, 2021.

Hutchinson, Thomas. *The History of Massachusetts, from the First Settlement Thereof in 1628, until the Year 1750.* 3rd ed. Vol. 2. Salem, MA: Printed by Thomas C. Cushing, for Thomas and Andrews, Boston, 1795, babel.hathitrust.org/cgi/pt?id=nyp.33433115689857&view= 1up&seq=2.

Irving, Washington. "Philip of Pokanoket." *The Sketch Book of Geoffrey Crayon, Gent.* 2nd ed. Vol. 2. London: John Murray, 1820, pp. 237–74, books.google.com/books?id= aMLxCOhDvAAC&printsec=frontcover&dq=Irving+Sketch+Book+Pokanoket+ 1820&hl=en&newbks=1&newbks_redir=0&sa=X&ved=2ahUKEwj46O-6tc7tAhX XGs0KHYkuANAQ6AEwAXoECAUQAg#v=onepage&q=Irving%20Sketch%20 Book%20Pokanoket%201820&f=false.

Jackson, Holly. "'So We Die before Our Own Eyes': Willful Sterility in *The Country of the Pointed Firs.*" *New England Quarterly*, vol. 82, no. 2, 2009, pp. 264–84, www.jstor.org/ stable/25652008. Accessed Sep. 10, 2021.

Jackson, Shirley. *Hangsaman.* Farrar, Straus and Young, 1951.

———. *The Haunting of Hill House.* 1959. Penguin, 1986.

———. *Life among the Savages: An Uneasy Chronicle.* Farrar, Straus and Young, 1953.

———. *The Lottery; or, The Adventures of James Harris.* Farrar, Straus, 1949.

———. *Raising Demons.* Farrar, Straus and Cudahy, 1957.

———. *We Have Always Lived in the Castle.* Viking, 1962.

Jacobs, Harriet A. *Incidents in the Life of a Slave Girl. Written by Herself.* 1861, edited by Lydia Maria Child, docsouth.unc.edu/fpn/jacobs/jacobs.html.

James, Henry. *The Bostonians: A Novel.* 2 vols. 1886. Macmillan, 1921, books.google.com/ books?id=sfhaAAAAMAAJ&newbks=1&newbks_redir=0&source=gbs_navlinks_s.

Jamneck, Lynne, editor. *Dreams from the Witch House: Female Voices of Lovecraftian Horror.* Dark Regions Press, 2015.

Jefferson, Thomas. "A Summary View of the Rights of British America." *The Papers of Thomas Jefferson*, avalon.law.yale.edu/18th_century/jeffsumm.asp.

Jewett, Sarah Orne. *The Country of the Pointed Firs.* 1896. Houghton Mifflin, 1910, catalog. hathitrust.org/Record/100319827.

———. "The Foreigner." *Atlantic Monthly*, vol. 86, no. 514, 1900, pp. 152–67.

———. "Miss Tempy's Watchers." *Atlantic Monthly*, vol. 61, no. 365, 1888, pp. 289–95.

[Johnson, Edward]. *Johnson's Wonder-Working Providence 1628–1651*, edited by J. Franklin Jameson, Original Narratives of Early American History, Charles Scribner's Sons, 1910, library.si.edu/digital-library/book/johnsonswonderw00john.

Joshi, S. T. *I Am Providence: The Life and Times of H. P. Lovecraft*. 2 vols. Hippocampus Press, 2010.

———, editor. *H.P. Lovecraft: Four Decades of Criticism*. Ohio UP, 1980.

Josselyn, John. *An Account of Two Voyages to New-England, Made during the Years, 1638, 1663*. 1674. Boston: William Veazie, 1865, content.wisconsinhistory.org/digital/collection/aj/id/9139.

Karlsen, Carol. *The Devil in the Shape of a Woman: Witchcraft in Colonial New England*. Vintage Random House, 1989.

Karpinski, Joanne. "The Gothic Underpinnings of Realism in the Local Colorists' No Man's Land." *Frontier Gothic: Terror and Wonder at the Frontier in American Literature*, edited by David Mogen, Scott Patrick Sanders, and Joanne B. Karpinski, Fairleigh Dickinson UP, 1993, go-gale-com.uscga.idm.oclc.org/ps/i.do?p=LitRC&u=23266&id=GALE|H1420078418&v=2.1&it=r&sid=summon.

Kiernan, Caitlin R. *The Red Tree*. Penguin Random House, 2009.

———. "So Runs the World Away." *The Mammoth Book of Vampire Stories by Women*, edited by Stephen Jones, Carroll & Graf, 2001, pp. 537–55.

King, Stephen. *Bag of Bones*. Scribner, 1990.

———. *Carrie*. Doubleday, 1974.

———. "Graveyard Shift." 1970. *Night Shift*. Signet/NAL, 1979, pp. 35–51.

———. *It*. Viking, 1986.

———. "The Man in the Black Suit." 1994. *Everything's Eventual: 14 Dark Tales*. Pocket Books, 2002, pp. 35–68.

———. *The Mist*. Dark Forces: New Stories of Suspense and Supernatural Horror, edited by Kirby McCauley, Viking, 1980.

———. *Pet Sematary*. Doubleday, 1983.

———. *Salem's Lot*. Signet/NAL, 1975.

———. *Stephen King's Danse Macabre*. Berkley, 1983.

Kristeva, Julia. *Powers of Horror: An Essay on Abjection*. Translated by Leon S. Roudiez, Columbia UP, 1982.

Landsberg, Alison. "Horror Vérité: Politics and History in Jordan Peele's *Get Out* (2017)." *Continuum*, vol. 32, no. 5, 2018, pp. 629–42, doi:10.1080/10304312.2018.1500522.

Larcom, Lucy. *Wild Roses of Cape Ann, and Other Poems*. Boston: Houghton Mifflin, 1880, books.google.com/books?id=H8MvAQAAIAAJ&newbks=1&newbks_redir=0&dq=Lucy+Larcom+Mistress+Hale+of+Beverly+Wild+Roses+of+Cape+Ann&source=gbs_navlinks_s.

LaValle, Victor. *The Ballad of Black Tom*. Tor, 2016.

Lepore, Jill. *The Name of War: King Philip's War and the Origins of American Identity*. Vintage, 1999.

Let's Scare Jessica to Death. Directed by John D. Hancock. Paramount Pictures, 1971.

Levin, Harry. *The Power of Blackness: Hawthorne, Poe, Melville*. Vintage, 1958.

Liz Duffy Adams: Playwright. lizduffyadams.com/about. Accessed Sep. 10, 2021.

Lloyd-Smith, Allan. "Nineteenth-Century American Gothic." *A Companion to the Gothic*, edited by David Punter, Blackwell, 2000, pp. 109–21.

———. "Nineteenth-Century American Gothic." *A New Companion to the Gothic*, edited by David Punter, Blackwell, 2012, pp. 163–75, onlinelibrary-wiley-com.uscga.idm.oclc.org/doi/10.1002/9781444354959.ch11.

Lockwood, J. Samaine. *Archives of Desire: The Queer Historical Work of New England Regionalism.* U of North Carolina P, 2015.

———. "Charlotte Perkins Gilman's Colonial Revival." *Legacy*, vol. 29, no. 1, 2012, pp. 86–114, *JSTOR*, www.jstor.org/stable/10.5250/legacy.29.1.0086. Accessed Sep. 10, 2021.

———. "Shopping for the Nation: Women's China Collecting in Late-Nineteenth-Century New England." *New England Quarterly*, vol. 81, no. 1, 2008, pp. 63–90, *JSTOR*, www.jstor.org/stable/20474604. Accessed Sep. 10, 2021.

Loewen, James W. *Sundown Towns: A Hidden Dimension of American Racism.* New Press, 2005.

Longfellow, Henry Wadsworth. *Giles Corey of the Salem Farms.* 1868. Houghton Mifflin, 1902, web.archive.org/web/20020831121611/http:/etext.lib.virginia.edu/etcbin/toccer-new2?id=LonCore.sgm&images=images/modeng&data=/texts/english/modeng/parsed&tag=public&part=all.

———. *Poems and Other Writings.* The Library of America, 2000.

———. *The Skeleton in Armor.* Boston: Osgood, 1877.

———. *Tales of a Wayside Inn.* Boston: Ticknor and Fields, 1863, www.gutenberg.org/files/25153/25153-h/25153-h.htm.

Lovecraft, H. P. *At the Mountains of Madness and Other Novels*, edited by S. T. Joshi, Arkham House, 1964 [Corrected sixth printing; *AMM*].

———. *The Case of Charles Dexter Ward*, edited by S. T. Joshi, U of Tampa P, 2010.

———. *Dagon and Other Macabre Tales*, edited by S. T. Joshi, Arkham House, 1965 [Corrected fifth printing; *Dagon*].

———. *The Dunwich Horror and Others*, edited by S. T. Joshi, Arkham House, 1963 [Corrected eighth printing; *DH*].

———. *Selected Letters 1 1911–1924*, edited by August Derleth and Donald Wandrei, Arkham House, 1965 [*SL* 1].

Lowell, Amy. "A Dracula of the Hills." *The Century Magazine*, June 1923, pp. 173–85, books.google.com/books?id=Z7cGAQAAIAAJ&pg=PA173&dq=Dracula+of+the+Hills+Lowell&hl=en&newbks=1&newbks_redir=0&sa=X&ved=2ahUKEwiwhbjVo6jtAhXqSTABHTn5Ae8Q6AEwA3oECAAQAg#v=onepage&q=Dracula%20of%20the%20Hills%20Lowell&f=false.

Lowell, Robert. *Lord Weary's Castle.* Harcourt, Brace, 1946, archive.org/details/lordwearyscastle0000unse/page/n5/mode/2up.

Lundie, Catherine A., editor. *Restless Spirits: Ghost Stories by American Women 1872–1926.* U of Massachusetts P, 1996.

MacKaye, Percy. *The Scarecrow, or the Glass of Truth: A Tragedy of the Ludicrous.* Macmillan, 1908, books.google.com/books?id=_C9BAQAAMAAJ&printsec=frontcover&dq=MacKaye,+Percy.+The+Scarecrow,+or+The+Glass+of+Truth:+A+Tragedy+of+the+Ludicrous&hl=en&newbks=1&newbks_redir=0&sa=X&ved=2ahUKEwjrvZSduYruAhUpvlkKHTgGAbYQ6AEwAHoECAEQAg#v=onepage&q=MacKaye%2C%20Percy.%20The%20Scarecrow%2C%20or%20The%20Glass%20of%20Truth%3A%20A%20Tragedy%20of%20the%20Ludicrous&f=false.

Magistrale, Tony. *Stephen King: America's Storyteller.* Praeger, 2010.

Mars, James. *Life of James Mars: A Slave Born and Sold in Connecticut.* Hartford: Case, Lockwood, 1869, books.google.com/books?id=Zvm7zg1SllsC&newbks=1&newbks_redir=0&source=gbs_navlinks_s.

Marsh, George Perkins. *The Goths in New-England: A Discourse Delivered at the Anniversary of the Philomathesian Society of Middlebury College, August 15, 1843.* Middlebury, 1843.

Martin, Phillip. "In the Age of Black Lives Matter, New England Faces Its Own Role In Slavery." Dec. 2, 2020. *GBH News*, www.wgbh.org/news/local-news/2020/12/02/in-the-age-of-black-lives-matter-new-england-faces-its-own-role-in-slavery. Accessed Sep. 10, 2021.

Mason, John. "A Brief History of the Pequot War (1736)," edited by Paul Royster, Electronic Texts in American Studies 42, digitalcommons.unl.edu/etas/42/.

Mather, Cotton. *Decennium Luctuosum. An History of Remarkable Occurrences, in the Long War, which New-England Hath Had with the Indian Savages, from the Year, 1688. To the Year 1698*. Boston, 1699, quod.lib.umich.edu/e/evans/N00725.0001.001/1:5.7?rgn=div2;view=fulltext.

———. *Magnalia Christi Americana or, the Ecclesiastical History of New England*. 1702. 2 vols. Hartford, 1855.

———. *The Short History of New-England* … Boston: B. Green, 1694, quod.lib.umich.edu/cgi/t/text/text-idx?c=eebo2;idno=A88931.0001.001.

———. *The Triumphs of the Reformed Religion, in America. The life of the renowned John Eliot a person justly famous in the church of God, not only as an eminent Christian, and an excellent Minister, among the English, but also, as a memorable evangelist among the Indians, of New-England; with some account concerning the late and strange success of the Gospel, in those parts of the world, which for many ages have lain buried in pagan ignorance*. Boston, 1691, name.umdl.umich.edu/N00446.0001.001.

Mather, Increase. *A Brief History of the Warr with the Indians in New-England*. An Online Electronic Text Edition. Boston, 1676, edited by Paul Royster, digitalcommons.unl.edu/cgi/viewcontent.cgi?article=1034&context=libraryscience.

———. "An Earnest Exhortation to the Inhabitants of New-England." Boston, 1676, edited by Reiner Smolinski, Electronic Texts in American Studies 31, digitalcommons.unl.edu/etas/31/.

———. *Remarkable Providences Illustrative of the Earlier Days of American Colonisation*, 1684, edited by George Offor, London: Reeves and Turner, 1890, catalog.hathitrust.org/Record/001408034/Home.

Melville, Herman. *Benito Cereno. The Piazza Tales*. New York: Dix & Edwards, 1856, pp. 110–271, www.gutenberg.org/files/15859/15859-h/15859-h.htm#toc_4.

———. "The Lightning-Rod Man." *The Piazza Tales*. New York: Dix & Edwards, 1856, pp. 272–87, www.gutenberg.org/files/15859/15859-h/15859-h.htm#toc_4.

———. *Moby-Dick*. New York: Harper & Brothers, 1851, catalog.hathitrust.org/Record/001423722.

———. "The Tartarus of Maids." 1855. *The Apple-Tree Table, and Other Sketches*. Princeton UP, 1922, pp. 184–210, catalog.hathitrust.org/Record/008589716.

Miller, Lewis H. "The Supernaturalism of Snow-Bound." *New England Quarterly*, vol. 53, no. 3, 1980, pp. 291–307, *JSTOR*, www.jstor.org/stable/365125. Accessed Sep. 10, 2021.

Mills, Daniel. *Moriah: A Novel*. ChiZine Publications, 2017.

Miller, Arthur. *The Crucible*. Viking Penguin, 1953.

Mitchell, Edward Page. "The Cave of the Splurgles." 1877, gutenberg.net.au/ebooks06/0606901h.html#s12.

———. "The Legendary Ship." *New York Sun*, May 17, 1885, p. 6, chroniclingamerica.loc.gov/data/batches/nn_dante_ver01/data/sn83030272/00175044863/1885051701/0092.pdf. Accessed Sep. 10, 2021.

———. "The Terrible Voyage of the Toad." *New York Sun*, Oct. 20, 1878, p. 2, chroniclingamerica.loc.gov/data/batches/nn_carson_ver02/data/sn83030272/00206533511/1878102001/0931.pdf. Accessed Sep. 10, 2021.

Mitchell, Isaac. *The Asylum: Or, Alonso and Melissa. An American Tale, Founded on Fact.* 2 vols. Poughkeepsie: Joseph Nelson, 1811.

Moreno-Garcia, Silvia, and Paula R.Stiles, editors. *She Walks in Shadows.* Innsmouth Free Press, 2015.

Morrison, A. B. *Spiritualism and Necromancy.* New York: Nelson and Phillips, 1873. books. google.com/books?id=XusRAAAAYAAJ&printsec=frontcover&dq=Morrison,+A.B.++Spiritualism+and+Necromancy&hl=en&newbks=1&newbks_redir=0&sa=X&ved=2ahUKEwi_nt6Nz4ruAhVeGVkFHZWmBG0QuwUwAHoECAEQBg#v=onepage&q=Morrison%2C%20A.B.%20%20Spiritualism%20and%20Necromancy&f=false.

Morrison, Toni. *Playing in the Dark: Whiteness and the Literary Imagination.* Vintage Random House, 1992.

Morton, Thomas. *The New English Canaan of Thomas Morton.* 1637, edited by Charles Francis Adams, Prince Society, 1883, library.si.edu/digital-library/book/newenglishcanaa00mort.

Murphy, Bernice M. "'The People of the Village Have Always Hated Us': Shirley Jackson's New England Gothic." *Short Story Criticism*, edited by Lawrence J. Trudeau, vol. 256, Gale, 2018. *Gale Literature Resource Center*, link.gale.com/apps/doc/H1420124822/LitRC?u=23266&sid=summon&xid=53fa7106. Accessed Sep. 10, 2021. Originally published in *Shirley Jackson*, edited by Bernice M. Murphy, McFarland, 2005, pp. 104–26.

———. *The Rural Gothic in American Popular Culture: Backwoods Horror and Terror in the Wilderness.* Palgrave Macmillan, 2013.

Neal, John. *Rachel Dyer: A North American Story.* Portland: Shirley and Hyde, 1828, books. google.com/books?id=WQ-5AQAACAAJ&source=gbs_navlinks_s.

[———]. "David Whicher: A North American Story." *The Token, for 1832*, edited by Samuel G. Goodrich, Boston: Gray & Bowen, 1832, pp. 349–72, babel.hathitrust.org/cgi/pt?id=hvd.32044011233574&view=1up&seq=22.

[———]. *Keep Cool, a Novel. Written in Hot Weather. By Somebody, M. D. C. &c. &c. &c Author of Sundry Works of Great Merit … Never Published, or Read, from His-story.* Baltimore: J. Cushing, 1817, babel.hathitrust.org/cgi/pt?id=uc1.31175023750501&view=1up&seq=13.

Nelson, Marilyn. *Fortune's Bones: The Manumission Requiem.* Front Street, 2004.

Norton, Charles Eliot. "Reminiscences of Old Cambridge." *The Cambridge Historical Society Publications I. Proceedings June 19, 1905-April 24, 1906.* Published by the Society, 1906, pp. 11–23, books.google.com/books?id=h4ElAQAAMAAJ&newbks=1&newbks_redir=0&dq=Charles+Eliot+Norton++%E2%80%9CReminiscences+of+Old+Cambridge%22&source=gbs_navlinks_s.

Norton, Mary Beth. *In the Devil's Snare: The Salem Witchcraft Crisis of 1692.* Knopf, 2002.

Nunes, Rachel. "Just 'Rhode Island': Voters Ax Providence Plantations." *Patch* 5 Nov. 2020, patch.com/rhode-island/cranston/just-rhode-island-voters-ax-providence-plantations. Accessed Sep. 10, 2021.

O'Brien, Jean. "'Vanishing' Indians in Nineteenth-Century New England: Local Historians' Erasure of Still-Present Indian Peoples." *New Perspectives on Native North America: Cultures, Histories, and Representations*, edited by Sergei Kan, Pauline Turner, and Raymond Fogelson, U of Nebraska P, 2006, pp. 414–32.

Ofgang, Erik. "The Mystery of a Connecticut 'Vampire' Has Been Solved." *Connecticut Magazine.* October 2019, www.connecticutmag.com/history/the-mystery-of-a-connecticut-vampire-has-been-solved/article_043e33c2-d4c6-11e9-80a6-1b717e11b783.html?fbclid=IwAR3K0WHexOANzAJF3SGL8VSEjQWuRllUCk5PevHfYlby72Z-f92BXifJXbk. Accessed 10 Sept. 2021.

Okorafor, Nnedi. "Lovecraft's Racism and the World Fantasy Award Statuette." *Nnedi's Wahala Zone Blog*, Dec. 14, 2011, nnedi.blogspot.com/2011/12/lovecrafts-racism-world-fantasy-award.html. Accessed Sept. 10, 2021.

Okorafor-Mbachu, Nnedi. "Stephen King's Super-Duper Magical Negroes." *Strange Horizons*, Oct. 25, 2004, web.archive.org/web/20061114013842/http:/www.strangeh orizons.com/2004/20041025/kinga.shtml. Accessed Sep. 10, 2021.

Olcott, Henry Steel. *People from the Other World.* Hartford: American Publishing, 1875, books. google.com/books?id=ruzy2w1ba0kC&printsec=frontcover&dq=Olcott,+Henry+ Steel.+People+from+the+Other+World&hl=en&newbks=1&newbks_redir=0&sa= X&ved=2ahUKEwjG9oKz34ruAhVLXc0KHWGHCKMQuwUwAHoECAEQB g#v=onepage&q=Olcott%2C%20Henry%20Steel.%20People%20from%20the%20 Other%20World&f=false.

O'Neill, Eugene. *Desire under the Elms.* Boni & Liveright, 1925.

ParaNorman. Directed and written by Chris Butler. Focus Features, 2012.

Paglia, Camille. *Sexual Personae.* Vintage Random House, 1990.

Painter, Nell Irvin. *The History of White People.* Norton, 2010.

Palmer, Paulina. *Lesbian Gothic: Transgressive Fictions.* Cassell, 1999.

Patton, Elizabeth A. "*Get Out* and the Legacy of Sundown Suburbs in Post-Racial America." *New Review of Film and Television Studies*, vol. 17, no. 3, pp. 349–63, doi:10.1080/ 17400309.2019.1622889. Accessed Sep. 10, 2021.

Peattie, Elia. "The Crime of Micah Rood." *Cosmopolitan*, vol. 4, no. 5, 1888, pp. 383–89, www. google.com/books/edition/The_Cosmopolitan/rt_KYpMkrVoC?hl=en&gbpv= 1&dq=Peattie+Crime+of+Micah+Rood&pg=PA383&printsec=frontcover#v= onepage&q=Micah%20Rood&f=false.

Peele, Jordan, director. *Get Out.* Universal Pictures, 2017.

Petry, Ann. *Tituba of Salem Village.* 1964. Harper Collins, 1991.

Phelps, Elizabeth Stuart. *The Gates Ajar.* 1868. Boston: Fields, Osgood, 1869, books.google. com/books?id=7oMEAAAAYAAJ&newbks=1&newbks_redir=0&dq=Phelps+The+ Gates+Ajar&source=gbs_navlinks_s.

———. "Since I Died." *Scribner's Monthly Magazine*, Feb. 1873, pp. 449–52, babel.hathitrust. org/cgi/pt?id=coo.31924079633214&view=1up&seq=455&q1=Phelps.

Poe, Edgar Allan. *Eureka—a Prose Poem.* 1848, xroads.virginia.edu/~Hyper/POE/eureka. html.

———. *Tales of the Grotesque and Arabesque.* 2 vols. Philadelphia: Lea and Blanchard, 1840, docsouth.unc.edu/southlit/1840poe1/1840poe1.html.

Pringle, James R. *History of the Town and City of Gloucester, Cape Ann, Massachusetts.* Gloucester, 1892, www.google.com/books/edition/History_of_the_Town_and_City_of_Gloucest/ tkY9AAAAYAAJ?hl=en&gbpv=1&dq=inauthor:%22James+Robert+ Pringle%22&printsec=frontcover.

Pyle, Howard. "The Salem Wolf." *Harper's Monthly Magazine*, Dec. 1909, pp. 1–12,books. google.com/books?id=y94_AQAAMAAJ&pg=PA3&dq=Harper%27s+Monthly+ Magazine+The+Salem+Wolf&hl=en&newbks=1&newbks_redir=0&sa=X&ved= 2ahUKEwj8oLSprMTtAhWRylkKHZYfDwMQ6AEwAnoECAIQAg#v= onepage&q&f=false.

Reynolds, David. *Beneath the American Renaissance: The Subversive Imagination in the Age of Emerson and Melville.* Harvard UP, 1988.

Rhode Island Slave History Medallions: Documenting Places and People in the History of Slavery in Rhode Island, rishm.org. Accessed Sep. 10, 2021.

Richards, Eliza. *Gender and the Poetics of Reception in Poe's Circle*. Cambridge UP, 2004.

Ringe, Donald. *American Gothic: Imagination and Reason in Nineteenth-Century Fiction*. UP of Kentucky, 1982.

Ringel, Faye. "'Diabolists and Decadents': Lovecraft's Gothic Puritans." *Lit: Literature Interpretation Theory*, vol. 5, no. 1, 1994, pp. 45–51.

———. *New England's Gothic Literature: History and Folklore of the Supernatural from the Seventeenth through the Twentieth Centuries*. Edwin Mellen Press, 1995.

Ringel, Faye, and Jenna Randall. "Lovecraft for the Little Ones: *ParaNorman*, Plushies, and More." *Lovecraftian Proceedings 2*, edited by Dennis P. Quinn, Hippocampus Press, 2017, pp. 225–36.

Roberts, Kenneth. "Plain Remarks on Immigration for Plain Americans." *Saturday Evening Post*, Feb. 12, 1921, pp. 21+, babel.hathitrust.org/cgi/pt?id=uiug.30112109617230&view=1up&seq=594&skin=2021. Accessed Sep. 10, 2021.

———. *Why Europe Leaves Home*. Bobbs-Merrill, 1922, www.google.com/books/edition/Why_Europe_Leaves_Home/Ni2OAAAAMAAJ?hl=en&gbpv=1&dq=Roberts+Europe+Leaves+Home&printsec=frontcover.

Roberts, Sian Silyn. "A Transnational Perspective on American Gothic Criticism." *Transnational Gothic: Literary and Social Exchanges in the Long Nineteenth Century*, edited by Monika Elbert, Routledge, 2016, pp. 19–34.

Romano, Aja. "Lovecraftian Horror—and the Racism at Its Core—Explained: H.P. Lovecraft Was One of the Most Influential Writers of the 20th Century. He Was Also One of Its Most Racist." *Vox*, Aug. 18, 2020, www.vox.com/culture/21363945/hp-lovecraft-racism-examples-explained-what-is-lovecraftian-weird-fiction?fbclid=IwAR2D_VNAajpgTJAzEkgtAPwX4B9UC9vdaGxLuECp06BhNJ1-DwhvMCvg-ikVox. Accessed Sep. 10, 2021.

Roosevelt, Theodore. "Address." *Report of the National Congress of Mothers: Held in the City of Washington, D. C., March 10–17, 1905*. catalog.hathitrust.org/Record/000458430.

Rosenthal, Bernard. *Salem Story: Reading the Witch Trials of 1692*. Cambridge UP, 1995.

Rowlandson, Mary. *Narrative of the Captivity and Restoration of Mrs. Mary Rowlandson*. 1675, www.gutenberg.org/files/851/851-h/851-h.htm.

Ruff, Matt. *Lovecraft Country*. HarperCollins, 2016.

Salmonson, Jessica Amanda, editor. *What Did Miss Darrington See? An Anthology of Feminist Supernatural Fiction*. The Feminist Press, 1989.

Sargent, Epes. *Peculiar: A Tale of the Great Transition*. New York: Carleton, 1863, www.google.com/books/edition/PECULIAR_A_Tale_of_the_Great_Transition/9HLKKhfqOiIC?hl=en&gbpv=1&bsq=Sargent.

[———]. *Planchette; or, The Despair of Science*. Boston: Roberts, 1869, books.google.com/books?id=d3l-Ft9Yg2AC&printsec=frontcover&dq=Planchette;+or,+The+Despair+of+Science&hl=en&newbks=1&newbks_redir=0&sa=X&ved=2ahUKEwiH6Oi22IruAhUHGVkFHYd5DegQuwUwAHoECAIQBQ#v=onepage&q=Planchette%3B%20or%2C%20The%20Despair%20of%20Science&f=false.

The Scarecrow. Directed by Boris Sagal. Hollywood Television Theater, 1972.

Scottow, Joshua. *A NARRATIVE Of The Planting of the Massachusets COLONY Anno 1628 … 1694*, edited by Paul Royster, Joshua Scottow Papers. Libraries at University of Nebraska-Lincoln, digitalcommons.unl.edu/scottow/4/.

Sedgwick, Catherine Maria. *A New-England Tale; or, Sketches of New-England Character and Manners*. 1822, edited by Victoria Clements, Oxford UP, 1995.

————. "Slavery in New England." *Bentley's Miscellany*, vol. 34, 1853, pp. 417–24, books. google.com/books?id=8-ARAAAAYAAJ&printsec=frontcover&dq=Slavery+in+ New+England+Bentley%E2%80%99s+Miscellany+34+1853&hl=en&newbks= 1&newbks_redir=0&sa=X&ved=2ahUKEwiq-8Hh2YruAhWbEFkFHfmOA9kQ6A EwAXoECAMQAg#v=onepage&q=New%20England&f=false.

Sephton, Rev. John, translator. *Eirik the Red's Saga: A Translation*. Liverpool: D. Marples, 1880, books.google.com/books?id=rdS1RFM8iuEC&newbks=1&newbks_redir= 0&dq=Sephton+Eirik+the+Red%27s+Saga&source=gbs_navlinks_s.

The Shirley Jackson Awards. www.shirleyjacksonawards.org/. Accessed Sep. 10, 2021.

Sigourney, Lydia. "Fall of the Pequod." *Myrtis with Other Etchings and Sketchings*. New York: Harper and Bros., 1846, pp. 101–38, books.google.com/books?id=pKA1AAAAMAAJ& newbks=1&newbks_redir=0&source=gbs_navlinks_s.

————. *Illustrated Poems*. Philadelphia: Carey and Hart, 1849, quod.lib.umich.edu/cgi/t/ text/text-idx?c=amverse;idno=BAD9857.0001.001.

————. *Selected Poems*. Philadelphia: Biddle, 1845, books.google.com/books?id=2bs_ AAAAYAAJ&newbks=1&newbks_redir=0&printsec=frontcover#v=onepage&q&f= false.

————. *The Western Home, and Other Poems*. Philadelphia: Parry and McMillan, 1854, books. google.com/books?id=9k6dL0Li98MC&newbks=1&newbks_redir=0&printsec= frontcover&source=gbs_ge_summary_r&cad=0#v=onepage&q&f=false.

Simmons, William S. *Spirit of the New England Tribes: Indian History and Folklore, 1620–1984*. UP of New England, 1986.

Skinner, Charles M. *American Myths and Legends*. Vol. 1. Lippincott, 1903, books.google.com/ books?id=C_-AAAAAMAAJ&vq=Mast+Swamp&source=gbs_navlinks_s.

Slosson, Annie Trumbull. "A Dissatisfied Soul." Lundie, pp. 284–99.

————. "Dumb Foxglove." *Dumb Foxglove and Other Stories*. New York: Harper and Bros., 1898, pp. 3–46, books.google.com/books?id=oXopAQAAIAAJ&vq=Contents&source= gbs_navlinks_s.

"A Speakin Ghost." *Seven Dreamers*. New York: Harper and Bros., 1890, pp. 237–81, books. google.com/books?id=0lsUAAAAYAAJ&source=gbs_navlinks_s.

Smith, Elizabeth Oakes. *Shadow Land, or, The Seer*. New York: Fowlers and Wells, 1852, books. google.com/books?id=VfcvAAAAYAAJ&newbks=1&newbks_redir=0&source=gbs_ navlinks_s.

Speare, Elizabeth George. *The Witch of Blackbird Pond*. 1958. Houghton Mifflin Harcourt, 2011.

Spofford, Harriet Prescott. "The Amber Gods." *The Amber Gods and Other Stories*. Boston: Ticknor and Fields, 1863, pp. 1–66, books.google.com/books?id=2LQEcdPqFroC& newbks=1&newbks_redir=0&vq=Asian+imp&dq=Spofford+Circumstance&source= gbs_navlinks_s.

————. "Circumstance." *The Amber Gods and Other Stories*, pp. 153–72.

————. "Her Story." Lundie, pp. 217–34.

————. *A Little Book of Friends*. Little, Brown, 1916, babel.hathitrust.org/cgi/pt?id= pst.000031416474&view=1up&seq=7.

Stannard, Ed. "Slavery in Connecticut, Ended Only in 1848, Had a Long History." *Connecticut Magazine*, June 19, 2020, www.connecticutmag.com/history/slavery-in- connecticut-ended-only-in-1848-had-a-long-history/article_09d8cc16-b23d-11ea- 8a6f-6fa1d7785f53.html. Accessed Sep. 10, 2021.

Stern, Madeleine, editor. *Behind a Mask: The Unknown Thrillers of Louisa May Alcott*. William Morrow, 1975.

Stetson, George. "The Animistic Vampire in New England." *American Anthropologist*, vol. 9, no. 1, 1896, pp. 1–13.

Stinson, Susan. *Spider in a Tree: A Novel of the First Great Awakening*. Small Beer Press, 2013.

Stowe, Harriet Beecher. *Oldtown Fireside Stories*. Boston: James R. Osgood, 1872, archive. org/details/cu31924022182418/page/n11/mode/2up.

———. *Oldtown Folks*. Boston: Fields, Osgood, 1869, books.google.com/books?id= NekRAAAAYAAJ&newbks=1&newbks_redir=0&source=gbs_navlinks_s.

———. *Uncle Tom's Cabin: Or, Life among the Lowly*. Boston: John P. Jewett, 1852, books. google.com/books?id=vyVDAQAAMAAJ&printsec=frontcover&source=gbs_ge_ summary_r&cad=0#v=onepage&q=Authentic%20Ghost&f=false.

Sword, Helen. *Ghostwriting Modernism*. Cornell UP, 2002.

Tartt, Donna. *The Secret History*. Knopf, 1992.

Taylor, John M. *The Witchcraft Delusion in Colonial Connecticut*. 1908. Corner House Publishers, 1974, www.gutenberg.org/files/12288/12288-h/12288-h.htm.

Tenney, Del, producer. *Psychomania* [*Violent Midnight*]. Victoria Films, 1963.

Thaxter, Celia. *The Cruise of the Mystery and Other Poems*. Boston: Houghton, Mifflin, 1886, books.google.com/books?id=vXs1AAAAMAAJ&vq=Mystery&dq=The+Cruise+of+ the+Mystery+and+Other+Poems&source=gbs_navlinks_s.

Thompson, D. P. [Daniel Pierce]. *Locke Amsden*. 1847. Boston: Hall and Whiting, 1881, www.google.com/books/edition/Locke_Amsden_Or_the_Schoolmaster_a_Tale/ ZPI2AQAAIAAJ?hl=en&gbpv=1.

———. *Lucy Hosmer, or, The Guardian and Ghost*. Burlington: C. Goodrich & S.B. Nichols, 1848, www.google.com/books/edition/Lucy_Hosmer_Or_The_Guardian_and_Ghost/ AqJUAAAAYAAJ?hl=en&gbpv=1.

Todorov, Tzvetan. *Introduction a la littérature fantastique*. Editions du Seuil, 1970.

Tomlinson, R. G., *Witchcraft Trials of Connecticut: The First Comprehensive, Documented History of Witchcraft Trials in Colonial Connecticut*. Privately printed, 1978.

"Transformation." Directed by Barbara Hirschfeld. 1972. vimeo.com/channels/ vtarchivemovieproject/153425994.

Tremblay, Paul. *A Head Full of Ghosts*. William Morrow, 2015.

———. *Survivor Song*. Titan Books, 2020.

Truffin, Sherry R. "'Gigantic Paradox, Too ... Monstrous for Solution': Nightmarish Democracy and the Schoolhouse Gothic from 'William Wilson' to *The Secret History*." Crow, pp. 164–75.

Tryon, Thomas. *Harvest Home*. Knopf, 1973.

Tylor, Edward B. *Primitive Culture: Researches into the Development of Mythology, Philosophy, Religion, Art, and Custom*. Vol. 1. London: John Murray, 1871, books.google.com/ books?id=AucLAAAAIAAJ&newbks=1&newbks_redir=0&dq=1+E.+B.+Tylor,+ Primitive+Culture:+Researches+into+the+Development+of+Mythology,&source= gbs_navlinks_s.

Ungerer, Walter, director, writer, and producer. *Solstice*. 1971.

———, director and producer. *The Animal*. 1976. Dark Horse Films DVD, 2009.

Walker, Francis A. "Immigration and Degradation." *Forum*, vol. 11, Aug. 1891, pp. 634–44. books.google.com/books?id=KPoLAAAAMAAJ&newbks=1&newbks_redir=0&dq= The+Forum+August+1891+Francis+Amasa+Walker&source=gbs_navlinks_s.

Wallace, Diana, and Andrew Smith, editors. *The Female Gothic: New Directions*. Palgrave Macmillan, 2009.

Wardrop, Daneen. *Emily Dickinson's Gothic: Goblin with A Gauge*. U of Iowa P, 1996.

Watters, David H. "Revising New England: Self-Portraits of a Region." *Colby Quarterly*, vol. 39, no.1, 2003, pp. 10–25, digitalcommons.colby.edu/cgi/viewcontent.cgi?article= 3395&context=cq. Accessed Sep. 10, 2021.

Weierman, Karen Woods. "'A Slave Story I Began and Abandoned': Sedgwick's Antislavery Manuscript." *Catherine Maria Sedgwick: Critical Perspectives*, edited by Lucinda L. Damon-Bach and Victoria Clements, Northeastern UP, 2003, pp.122–40.

Weinstock, Jeffrey Andrew. *Charles Brockden Brown*. Gothic Authors: Critical Revisions. U of Wales P, 2011.

———. *Scare Tactics: Supernatural Fiction by American Women*. Fordham UP, 2008.

Weinstock, Jeffrey Andrew, editor. *The Monster Theory Reader*. U of Minnesota P, 2020.

Wester, Maisha L. *African American Gothic: Screams from Shadowed Places*. Palgrave Macmillan, 2012.

———. "Black Diasporic Gothic." Wester and Reyes, pp. 289–303.

Wester, Maisha, and Xavier Aldana Reyes, editors. *Twenty-First-Century Gothic: An Edinburgh Companion*. Edinburgh University Press, 2019. *JSTOR*, www.jstor.org/stable/10.3366/ j.ctvnjbgx9. Accessed Sep. 10, 2021.

Wharton, Edith. *A Backward Glance*. 1934, A Project Gutenberg of Australia eBook. gutenberg.net.au/ebooks02/0200271.txt.

———. "Bewitched." *Here and Beyond*. 1925, D. Appleton, 1926, gutenberg.net.au/ ebooks06/0606991h.html#s3.

———. *Ethan Frome*. 1911. Charles Scribner's, 1919, books.google.com/books?id= 8PBLAQAAMAAJ&newbks=1&newbks_redir=0&dq=Wharton,+Edith.+Ethan+ Frome&source=gbs_navlinks_s.

———. *Summer: A Novel*. D. Appleton, 1917, books.google.com/books?id= 1GMeAAAAMAAJ&newbks=1&newbks_redir=0&dq=Wharton,+Edith.+ SUmmer&source=gbs_navlinks_s.

Whitman, Sarah Helen. *Edgar Poe and His Critics*. New York: Rudd & Carleton, 1860, books. google.com/books?id=-OgQcWin5yQC&printsec=frontcover&dq=Edgar+Poe+ and+His+Critics&hl=en&newbks=1&newbks_redir=0&sa=X&ved=2ahUKEwjH5 aLq3YruAhWYGs0KHd36AqIQ6AEwAXoECAIQAg#v=onepage&q=Edgar%20 Poe%20and%20His%20Critics&f=false.

———. *Hours of Life*. Providence: G. H. Whitney, 1853, catalog.hathitrust.org/Record/ 001027967.

Whittier, John Greenleaf. ———*Snow-Bound: A Winter Idyll*. 1865. Boston: Ticknor and Fields, 1866, books.google.com/books?id=WDzjpjCF7L4C&newbks=1&newbks_ redir=0&vq=copyright&dq=Whittier+Snow-Bound+1865&source=gbs_navlinks_s.

———. *The Supernaturalism of New England*, edited by Edward Wagenknecht, U of Oklahoma P, 1969.

———. *Whittier's Poems*. Household Edition. Boston: Houghton Mifflin, 1891.

Wigglesworth, Michael. *The Day of Doom, Or, a Poetical Description of the Great and Last Judgement*. 1662, www.gutenberg.org/files/56053/56053-h/56053-h.htm.

Wilkins [Freeman], Mary E. *Giles Corey, Yeoman*. New York: Harper and Bros., 1893, books. google.com/books?id=9IY0AAAAMAAJ&source=gbs_navlinks_s.

Wilkins Freeman, Mary E. "The Little Maid at the Door." *Silence and Other Stories*. New York: Harper and Bros., 1898, pp. 225–54, babel.hathitrust.org/cgi/pt?id=hvd. hwk6nm&view=1up&seq=8.

———. "Luella Miller." Lundie, pp. 305–16.

Wilkins-Freeman, Mary. *Collected Ghost Stories*, edited by Edward Wagenknecht, Arkham House, 1974.

Williams, William Carlos. *Tituba's Children. Many Loves and Other Plays; the Collected Plays of William Carlos Williams*. New Directions, 1961, pp. 225–300.

Winslow, W. S. *The Northern Reach*. Flatiron Books, 2021.

Winthrop, John. *Winthrop's Journal: "History of New England", 1630–1649. Original Narratives of American History*. Vol. 1. Scribners, 1908, archive.org/details/winthropsjournal00wint/page/n11/mode/2up.

———. *Winthrop's Journal: "History of New England", 1630–1649. Original Narratives of American History*. Vol. 2. Scribners, 1908, books.google.com/books?id=0D2lSuKkDmYC&source=gbs_navlinks_s.

The Witch: A New England Folktale. Directed and written by Robert Eggers. Rooks Nest Entertainment. 2015.

Witness Stones Project, Inc.: Restore History. witnessstonesproject.org/. Accessed Sep. 10, 2021.

[Wood, Sally S. B. K.]. *Julia, and the Illuminated Baron: A Novel Founded on Recent Facts which have Transpired in the course of the late Revolution of Moral Principles in France*. Portsmouth, New Hampshire: Oracle Press, 1800.

Woodward, P. H. "The Tradition of Micah Rood." *Papers of the New London County Historical Society*. Part 3. Vol. 1. New London, 1891, pp. 27–33, www.google.com/books/edition/Records_and_Papers_of_the_New_London_Cou/cVRMDpUh3RMC?kptab=editions&gbpv=1.

Woodward, Walter. *Prospero's America: John Winthrop, Jr., Alchemy, and the Creation of New England Culture, 1606–1676*. U of North Carolina P, 2010.

Wynne, Douglas. *Red Equinox*. JournalStone, 2015.

———. Direct message to the author. Jan. 25, 2021.

Wynne, Madeline Yale. *The Little Room and Other Stories*. 1895. 2nd ed., Way & Williams, 1906, books.google.com/books?id=Cm81AAAAMAAJ&newbks=1&newbks_redir=0&source=gbs_navlinks_s.

YellowBrickRoad. Directed and written by Jesse Holland and Andy Mitton. Points North Films, 2010.

Young, Helen. "Place and Time: Medievalism and Making Race." *The Year's Work in Medievalism*, vol. 28, 2013, pp. 1–6, sites.google.com/site/theyearsworkinmedievalism/all-issues/28-2013. Accessed Sep. 10, 2021.

———. *Race and Popular Fantasy Literature: Habits of Whiteness*. Routledge, 2015.

INDEX

CPSIA information can be obtained
at www.ICGtesting.com
Printed in the USA
BVHW072119030222
628053BV00005B/82